Dorothy Bromiley Phelan is Lancashire born, with textiles in her blood. Her father worked in the cotton industry and designed cotton bedspreads. Her mother was a Court dressmaker. As a young girl, she was regularly taken by her father to look at the needlework at Platt Hall, in her home city of Manchester. Having once been a contract film actress to Paramount Film Studios in Hollywood, she now lives with the writer Brian Phelan in Dorset and has two married children, Joshua Losey and Kate Grosjean.

Her knowledge of needlework is considerable. She is the author of *Florentine Canvaswork, A Practical Book of Patterns* (1991), and with Jerzy Kierkuc-Bielinski curated the highly successful 'The Needle's Excellency' exhibition of Stuart needleworks at the Holburne Museum, Bath, in 2000.

As well as curating and writing the catalogue for 'The Point of the Needle' exhibition, she is currently researching seventeenth century needlework designs for a book on antique raised and embossed needlework.

Following pages
A detail from a canvaswork book cover,
English School, after 1635 (see No. 12)

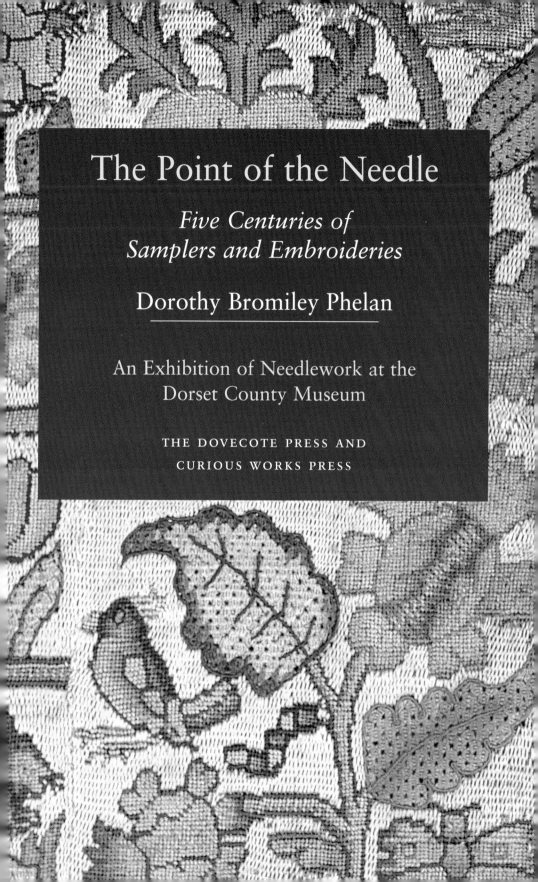

The Point of the Needle

*Five Centuries of
Samplers and Embroideries*

Dorothy Bromiley Phelan

An Exhibition of Needlework at the
Dorset County Museum

THE DOVECOTE PRESS AND
CURIOUS WORKS PRESS

An assortment of embroidery tools.
Including three English hallmarked silver bodkins, one engraved
'Wedg'd whole ages in a bodkin's eye'.

First published in 2001
to coincide with 'The Point of the Needle' Exhibition at
Dorset County Museum, Dorchester, Dorset DT1 1XA
Sponsored by Lawrence's Auctioneers of Crewkerne, Somerset

First published in the United Kingdom by
The Dovecote Press Ltd
Stanbridge, Wimborne, Dorset BH21 4JD

First published in the United States of America by
Curious Works Press
106 LeGrand Boulevard
Greenville, South Carolina 29607

BRITISH ISBN 1 874336 97 0
US ISBN 1 928584 04 7

Text Copyright © Dorothy Bromiley Phelan 2001

Dorothy Bromiley Phelan has asserted her rights
under the Copyright, Designs and Patent Act 1988
to be identified as author of this work

Typeset in Sabon
Designed by The Dovecote Press
Printed and bound by KHL Printing Co Pte Ltd, Singapore

A CIP catalogue record for this book is available
from the British Library

3 5 7 9 8 6 4 2

CONTENTS

ACKNOWLEDGEMENTS

The Trustees of the Dorset Natural History and Archaeological Society, owners of the Dorset County Museum, would like to thank Lawrence's Auctioneers of Crewkerne for their sponsorship of the Exhibition. They would also like to thank The Broderers Charity Trust and the Clothworkers' Foundation, whose donations have enabled the Royal School of Needlework to participate; the Worshipful Company of Needlemakers; the South West Museums Council and the Mansel-Pleydell Trustees for help with funding for conservation work, and the generous patrons and supporters listed below who have made the Exhibition possible.

Patrons: Jennifer Coombs, The Hon. Mrs Harriet Cotterell, Joanna Garnier, William Gronow Davis, Mr and Mrs Michael M.O. Jodrell, Mr and Mrs J.M. Kendall, Thomas B. Kyle, Anthony Pitt-Rivers, Mr and Mrs C. Pugh, The Simon Digby Charitable Trust, Guy and Valerie Smallwood, John and Sheila Stoller, Lady Anne Tree, Mr and Mrs Wilfrid Weld, Mrs G.E.S. Woodhouse. Supporters: Mr and Mrs Robin Garran, Mr and Mrs Ian Hay Davison, Sczerina Hichens, J.M.L. Hughes, Mrs Patricia Lidsey, Maureen Lipman, Lady Marriner, Mr and Mrs Peter Mayne, Mrs M.E. Russell, Sir Michael and Lady Turner, Sir Anthony Wilson. The Trustees would also like to thank the patrons and supporters who have chosen to remain anonymous.

The Museum's own collection of needlework has been augmented and enhanced by magnificent loans from a number of sources, and the Trustees would like to record their gratitude to Her Majesty The Queen, the Embroiderers' Guild, the Royal School of Needlework, Siva Swaminathan, the embroiderers who have created new work for the exhibition, and all the lenders who have generously allowed their work to be shown.

The Exhibition was curated by Dorothy Bromiley Phelan and designed by Astrid Garran. It was organized by Valerie Pitt-Rivers and Susan Bosanquet. A great many other people took part in planning, preparing items for exhibition and helping in numerous ways. Special mention must be made of Christopher Bosanquet; David Burnett; Elizabeth Elvin, Principal of the Royal School of Needlework; Helen Francis and her helpers; Joy Jarrett; Anthony Kilroy; Paul Lipscombe; Sharon Manitta; Kathy Staples; Lynn Szygenda and Amy Miller, respectively Curator and Assistant Curator at the Embroiderers' Guild; and Marilyn Wyatt.

INTRODUCTION

The opportunity to bring together a group of embroideries so diverse in technique, style, and purpose as those included in 'The Point of the Needle' Exhibition is a rare privilege. The selection is entirely personal, and is not intended to deliberately attempt a history of English embroidery. Its main source is the textile collection held by the Dorset County Museum. The museum opened in 1846, and the growth of the collection has largely been haphazard, principally by bequest, and often by the descendants of those who made them. Because of this, the needlework does reflect the major trends in the making of samplers, and other embroidery, from the early Stuart period to the present day, a span of more than four hundred years. If many of the items tell us a great deal about the evolution of design and technique in needlework, they have a far greater importance as works of art in their own right. Like all art they reflect both the society in which they were created, and the influences and preoccupations of their makers.

Most of the samplers in the Dorset County Museum collection have not been shown before. Although they are the exhibition's backbone, they share it with samplers that have been specially loaned: some historical, some modern, including the witty computer screen (No. 104) commissioned for the exhibition from apprentices at the Royal School of Needlework.

Other embroideries complement the samplers, displaying a wide selection, from Elizabeth I to Elizabeth II. Once again they range across the five centuries covered by the exhibition, and include clothing and small items of domestic wear; a coif head-dress and a night cap, fragments from a jacket, two waistcoats and an apron. But there are also small furnishings, such as a chair cover, and the sort of household objects that were once common in English houses – pincushions, a beaded tea cosy, book covers – as well as antique and modern raised work caskets, looking glass borders and silk and needlepoint panels. Some of the pieces were abandoned when unfinished, but even they provide a valuable insight into lost working methods, allowing us to 'unravel' and 'unpick' the techniques employed by their makers.

The earliest samplers were created by experienced embroiderers to record patterns and stitches, and by the novice as a progressively complicated needlework exercise and practice piece. Most early sampler patterns were for embroidering onto shirts, shifts, linen towels and the like. From the 1630s the emphasis changed radically. Large numbers of band pattern and spot motif samplers began to appear, mainly thanks to the introduction of French and Italian printed pattern books, and the arrival in England of immigrant craft workers fleeing religious persecution in continental Europe.

Few early pieces were signed, save for occasional initials, and only in the late eighteenth century do they begin to be inscribed with names and dates. Until then, women teaching needlework for a living probably had only a basic primary education, and taught alphabets copied from earlier needlework samples or from printed patterns. It is important to remember that with time embroidery worked its way down the social scale, eventually reaching the most disadvantaged of all, the institutionalized orphan (No. 84).

The opening of British and National schools throughout rural England in the mid nineteenth century led to a typically Victorian drive towards universal literacy. The sampler exchanged the parlour for the schoolroom, where it was used to teach basic numeracy and literacy skills. The colourful exuberance of Restoration and Georgian embroidery becomes a thing of the past. Lines of numbers and patiently-worked alphabets flow to and fro in tiny stitches. The change in priorities changed the appearance of the sampler. Designs were simplified, and restricted to cross stitch, with which the young were taught to copy sentimental moral and religious texts. By the 1880s sampler work was being described as 'the dying out of a practice by a process of degradation'. Ironically, the sampler had artistically become moribund whilst providing essential practical skills to the illiterate.

Yet the notion that these beautiful often fragile creations are survivors from a culture that is increasingly remote is not borne out by reality. One only has to look at the more recent twentieth century pieces, and all those made this year (Nos. 95-109), to realize that a fresh and more topical wind is blowing through the world of embroidery. Organisations such as the Royal School of Needlework and the Embroiderers' Guild, supported by the textile courses now being taught in many of Britain's art colleges, have inspired a renaissance amongst embroiderers that has breathed new life into it. Nor is it restricted only to women. The last piece in this book, and the exhibition, was worked by a man.

I said at the outset that needlework mirrored the world in which it was created. Because many of the pieces come from Dorset's county museum they have their origins in a rural county that happily remains nearly as unspoilt as when they were worked. The May Day revellers (No. 41) would have little difficulty following the steps of the country dances enjoyed at village fêtes today. The samplers known to be worked in Dorset provide a visual record of a world governed by the farming calendar, and which for many meant a life of hardship and struggle. Rarely does reality intrude. The eleven-year-old Mary Bradley's 1804 sampler (No. 47) is of her school, fields and neat lines of trees, yet she made it the year before the Battle of Trafalgar, when England was at war with Napoleonic France. A few years later Mary herself would probably have joined in the celebrations that ocasionally still took place in the remains of the ancient maze just outside her home village of Leigh.

One sampler that movingly evokes the precariousness of life in eighteenth century Dorset is the genealogical sampler of the Pleydell family (No. 35). It lists eight of the nine children born to Edmund Morton Pleydell (1724-1794) and his wife Anne. The Pleydells were Dorset landowners, and owners of two large country houses, but even they were not immune to tragedy. The lower half of the sampler is inscribed with the names of three of their four children who died when still young, one on the day of his birth, two others before the age of ten. Happily, the remaining empty space at the bottom of the sampler was never needed: indeed two of the surviving daughters lived well into their eighties. The sampler does leave a minor mystery unsolved. The one daughter not listed, Susannah, died in 1744, when Edmund was only twenty, and it may be that she was the result of a brief affair prior to his marriage, and thus never acknowledged.

Few samplers or embroideries can speak so eloquently of the circumstances surrounding their creation. Who, for example, would guess that the cottage and garden created by Constance Dickenson in 1942 (No. 91) were worked onto linen cut from a pair of shorts when she and her husband were separated and imprisoned by the Japanese in the notorious Changi Camp, Singapore?

Yet what the exhibition and this catalogue do illustrate is not only the time and dedication given to these embroideries, but the enjoyment gained by successive generations through working with the needle. Such treasures add immeasurably to the quality of our lives in ways undreamt of by their creators. Essentially 'The Point of the Needle' is an affirmation of life itself, a celebration of what skill and imagination can achieve with a small length of pointed steel:

> 'A Needle though it be but small and slender,
> Yet it is both a maker and a mender.'

A SCHOLE-HOUSE FOR THE NEEDLE
1585–1699

The first samplers to appear just before the end of the sixteenth century fall into two distinctive types, the spot sampler and the band sampler. A small, naturalistic scrolling pattern on a woman's head-dress and forehead cloth (No. 4) relates to a pattern on the spot motif sampler (No. 9), which evolved from the needlewoman's habit of recording interesting motifs. Broadly rectangular, these motifs were drawn from herbals and bestiaries.

The long and narrow shape of the band sampler (Nos. 13, 17, 18, 19, 20), with its horizontal, repeating patterns, echoes the format of a roll of manuscript or the prayer band that in medieval times was wrapped round womens' bodies during labour. Designed to teach the novice increasingly complex patterns and techniques, band samplers also celebrate the Elizabethan love of pattern. Although decorative they were not displayed, but stored rolled up. During the latter half of the seventeenth century, a girl's needlework education included working a casket or a looking glass border. These were worked in the most difficult of needlework techniques, the three-dimensional or raised work embroideries (Nos. 23, 25).

Despite the limited academic education of sixteenth and seventeenth century girls, their technical tuition included a wide range of needlework skills. The repertoire of stitches was extensive, enlivening patterns on articles as diverse as household linen (No. 6), personal items (No. 7), book bindings (No. 12), and caskets and looking glasses (Nos. 23, 24, 25). Designs were copied and modified from continental European and English pattern books of flora and fauna. These were either counted out, coloured and drawn out in black ink, or their outlines were pricked and pounced with dark or light powder. 'If your pleasure be', wrote one Tudor steward to his mistress, Lady Honor Lisle, 'I will make a painter take the pattern thereof, but it will be very busy because of a diversity of colours'. Guide marks are visible on the unfinished embroidered pattern on a night cap, probably started for a client by a paid needlewoman (No. 8).

4. COIF WITH CROSS-CLOTH. English School, 1585-1599.
Plain weave linen; silk thread, spangles, gilt and silver-gilt threads. Stitches include plaited braid, detached buttonhole, and backstitch.
Coif, 220 x 375 mm (8.5 x 15 in): cross-cloth, 340 x 245 x 235 mm (13.3 x 9.5 x 9.25 in) with attached textile.
The head-dress, which has been worn, is now opened out. The scrolling pattern encloses an Elizabethan summer nosegay of colourful English wild flowers and pale unripe fruit, diligently and 'curiously' worked, in the early meaning of assiduously. The fruit is forever under threat from marauding green woodpeckers, as is the eglantine rose from the worm. (Private Collection)

5. PILLOW COVER. English School, late sixteenth century.

Plain weave linen; silk thread, silver gilt thread, spangles. Stitches include satin, long and short, chain and plaited braid. 545 x 850 mm (21.5 x 32.5 in).

Such covers were originally known as pillow beres. The typical all-over scrolling design is airier and less dense than those on the coif and crosscloth on the previous page (No. 4) and the fragments of a woman's jacket (No. 7). The cover was dismantled from a cobbled-together white-painted wooden 1940s fire-screen, labelled: 'By an old ancestor Mitchaelbourne, Stanmer Park, Essex in 1700.' A bed cover with a similar pattern, but on a larger scale, is in the Victoria and Albert Museum (T222 1927). (Private Collection)

6. BURATO BORDER. Italian, about 1610.

Gauze weave cotton. Stitches include darning (Burato work), and button-hole. 65 x 270 mm (2.25 x 10.5 in).

The ground on which this border was worked is known as Burato, woven by twisting a pair of warp threads around a single weft. Bands such as this were used from the sixteenth century for decorating household and personal linen. This alternating symmetrical design, typical of Renaissance ornament, is similar to those in Vinciolo's 1587 pattern book of cutwork and lacis (meshed net, also known as filet lace). The designs were adapted and recorded on later seventeenth century band samplers. (Embroiderers' Guild Collection EG5380)

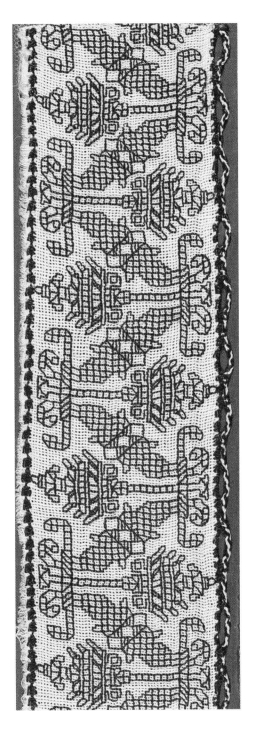

7. FRAGMENTS FROM A WOMAN'S JACKET. English School, 1620-30.
Plain weave linen; floss silk, silver, silver-gilt and wrapped silk metallic thread; spangles. Stitches include plaited braid, chain couching, trellis, stem, detached buttonhole. Each epaulette approx 250 x 125 mm (10 x 5 in).

Flowers, acorns and berries enclosed in scrolling vines adorn this trio of fragments, a sleeve and two shoulder guards or epaulettes. Each of the shoulder guards is embroidered with the same area of pattern, with an attention to matching details uncommon at this date. Contemporary jackets with similar designs are found in the Burrell Collection, Glasgow (29/127), and at the Victoria and Albert Museum, London (the Margaret Laton (1579-1662) jacket, T228-1994). (Private Collection)

8. MAN'S NIGHT CAP. Partially worked. English School, 1610-20.
Plain weave linen; silk thread, silver-gilt thread. Stitches include plaited braid, chain, detached buttonhole, satin, underside couching. 205 x 160 mm (8.5 x 6.25 in). Turn-back 55 mm (2.25 in).

This four-panelled night cap with seams was worn for informal wear and occasionally as part of regalia. The fact that the embroidery is unfinished provides the opportunity to see work-in-progress. On the fabric there is a slight trace of the under drawing, and a running stitch circle marks the flowerhead centres. Expert use of shading gives the appearance of applied layers, and padded effects are achieved by the use of satin stitch. This cap is unusual in that it is made up of four separate sections; most night caps were worked, or embroidered, on a single piece of linen. (Private Collection)

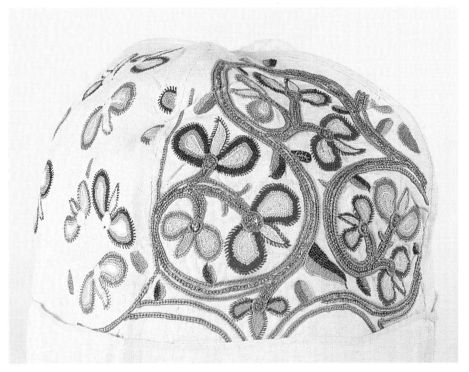

9. RANDOM SPOT SAMPLER. English School, 1630.
Plain weave linen; silk thread, metal thread. Stitches include eyelet, Queen, plaited braid, bullion knot, double cross, Montenegrin and tent. Selvedge upper and lower edges. 220 x 520 mm (8.5 x 21.5 in).
This sampler exhibits a wide repertoire of stitches and patterns, including several unusual motifs. Amongst these are the scroll design within a square, the floral emblems of the three kingdoms, and the royal cypher 'CR' for Charles I. This may be the earliest date for the appearance on an English sampler of a Jacobean couple holding hands. All these figures – biblical, mythological and secular – were shortly to become more common in needle-lace and other sampler designs, influenced by Richard Shorleyker's pattern book, *A Schole-House for the Needle* (1632). (Dorset County Museum 1917.8.2.)

10. CANVASWORK PANEL. English, 1635-55.
Linen canvas; silk thread. Stitches include tent worked in the half-cross method. 296 x 436 mm (11.5 x 17.5 in).
Although not signed or dated, this needlework is attributed, on reasonable authority, to Lucy Hutchinson (1620-after 1675) wife of Colonel John Hutchinson, a Puritan and parliamentary soldier, and signatory to the death-warrant of Charles I. A similar pastoral scene is in the Irwin Untermyer Collection, Metropolitan Museum, New York. Butterflies are said to refer to the Stuarts and the ironic symbolism may not have escaped Lucy Hutchinson's notice.

Dedicating a translation of a poem by Lucretius, Lucy Hutchinson wrote: 'I turned it into English in a roome where my children practizd the severall quallities they were taught, with their Tutors, & I numbred the sillables of my translation by the threds of the canvas I wrought in, & sett them downe with a pen & inke that stood by me'. (Private Collection)

12. *(Above)* CANVASWORK BOOK COVER. English School, 1640-50.
Linen canvas; wool yarn. Stitches include flat, tent, sloping gobelin and rococco. 200 x 260 x 42 mm (8 x 10.5 x 3 in).
An opportunity to compare the execution of a cover, by an amateur, with that of a professional (No. 11). The work has a pleasing symmetry, achieved by placing each element, on back and front, as its own mirror version; a subtlety made more obvious when the piece is flattened out. Possibly never mounted as a book cover, the 'gardener's heel', floral spots and other motifs also appear on satin groundings in Stuart narrative panels, taken from printed engravings such as *A Book of Beast Birds Flowers Fruits Flies and Worms* (1630). (Dorset County Museum 1953.172)

11. *(Opposite page)* EMBROIDERED BOOK BINDING. English School, after 1635.
Satin-weave silk; silk thread, vestigal ribbon attachments. Stitches include flat, tent, enroaching gobelin; and a variety of metal work techniques. 140 x 80 mm (5.5 x 3.25 in). Spine, 31mm (1.25 in).
Skilfully executed and probably a professional broderer's work. A white horseradish root sprouting greenery lies in a horizontal position at the base of the design, front and back. In an age favouring emblematic puzzles, this *impresa* (emblem) may have identified either designer or broderer, perhaps signifying the name Raifort or Radici. The book covered was *Tentations: Their Nature, Danger, Cure* by Richard Capel (2nd edition, 1635). (J.K. Wingfield-Digby Esq.,)

14. *(Left)* BAND SAMPLER. English School, 1650-60.
Plain weave linen; silk thread, metallic thread. Stitches include long-armed across, double running, satin, speckling, cross stitch variations and bullion. 544 x 163 mm (21.75 x 6.75 in).
Eight bands of formalised Italianate repeating patterns contrast with a highly-stylised female figure dressed in a farthingale. Evidently this is the work of a young novice, because she experienced some difficulty counting out the angle of the double-plait pattern arching over a carnation on the third band. (Siva Swaminathan Collection)

15. *(Opposite page)* CUTWORK AND NEEDLE-LACE BAND SAMPLER. English School, 1660s.
Plain weave linen; linen thread. Cutwork and needle-lace techniques. 510 x 165 mm (19.75 x 6.5 in).
Linen and linen threads were expensive, as now, and the novice was not spared more grounding textile than was absolutely essential for her practice piece. This worker was, however, highly skilled and the overall effect achieved is one of great delicacy.

Detached buttonhole, a needle-lace technique, was used to create the flower petals in the top band. Polychrome silk thread versions of this stitch were worked on many Stuart decorative embroideries (Burrell Collection 29/170, Glasgow). In the sixteenth century, it featured on items of domestic clothing (Nos. 4 & 7). Detached buttonhole became a component of the raised work panels contemporary with this piece. (Embroiderers' Guild Collection EG1982-7)

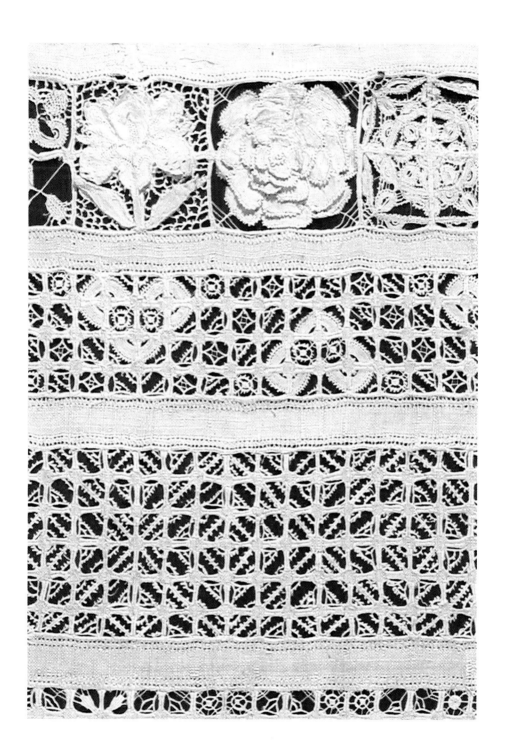

18. BAND SAMPLER. Partially worked. English School, 1657.
Plain weave linen; silk floss. Stitches include Holbein, Portuguese knotted stem, running, back, chain, cross, plaited braid, French knot. and an uncompleted band of cutwork. Selvedge at upper edge. 440 x 165 mm (17.5 x 6.25 in).

The patterned band immediately above the alphabet is an imitation of Burato work (No. 6). The date is followed by an enigmatic sequence of letters: 'a c d e i m'. This may derive from a series of vowel and consonant combinations known as the 'syllabary', and common to the horn-book, a child's portable elementary reading-aid already in use before the Stuart period. (Siva Swaminathan Collection)

19. BAND SAMPLER. 'Susanna Allen(s), work 1668'. English School.
Plain weave linen; silk thread, silver-gilt thread. Stitches include back, cross, long-armed cross, fishbone, long and short, satin, lattice and double running. No selvedges. 495 x 215 mm (19.5 x 8.5 in).
Predominant is a repeat pattern of honeysuckle flowers, alternating with a pineapple, placed upside down. The pineapple was then rare, and reputed to have first been grown in England for Charles II by the felicitously named Mr Rose, a royal gardener. An early English illustration of a pineapple appears in the frontispiece to John Parkinson's *Paradisi in Sole* (1629) depicting the Garden of Eden. The pattern, also seen worked in monochrome, is probably Italian. It is unlikely that so exotic a fruit would have been seen, or tasted by Susanna Allen. (Siva Swaminathan Collection)

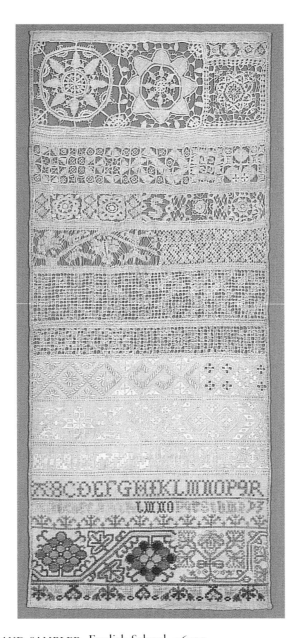

20. MIXED BAND SAMPLER. English School, 1670s.
Plain weave linen; silk thread, linen thread. Stitches include eyelet, cross, whitework, drawn thread, and filet. 520 x 219 mm (20.5 x 8.5 in).
The uppermost band is worked in a needle-lace technique with the glorious name of *Punto in Aria* (stitches in the air) taken from Italian pattern books published in the 1580s. Patterns with variations on the 's' symbol were common, but an initial seems to hover here. A rare configuration, the form of the letter 'x' interwoven with 'P', represents the Christian Chi-rho monogram standing for the first two letters of the name of Christ in Greek. (Royal School of Needlework)

[24]

21. CREWEL WORK SLIP. English School, 1670s.
Twill weave linen and cotton; crewel yarn. Stitches include straight, stem outline, back, and speckling. 243 x 274 mm (9.5 x 11 in).
The colours favoured for monochrome work were black, red or green, an effective technique used for domestic hangings and small panels, possibly inspired by engraved prints. The leopard is one of several slips worked on linen with irregularly-cut edges, before being applied to another grounding textile. The turning allowance between slips is remarkably economic. (Royal School of Needlework)

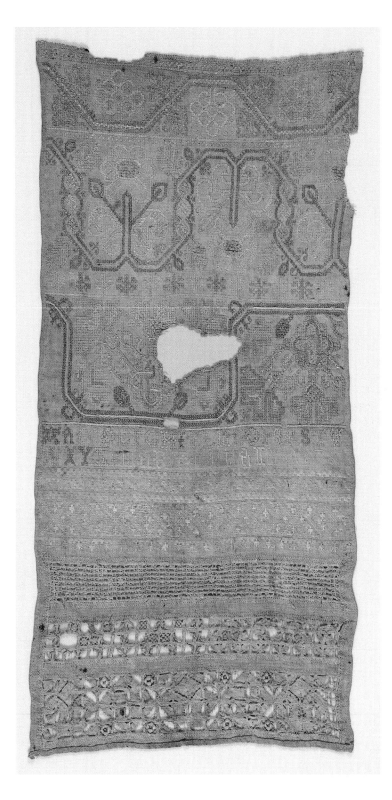

23. RAISED WORK CASKET. Initial 'M'. English School, after 1685.
Satin-weave silk; silk thread, metal thread, linen, metal braid, wax, mica, parchment, pearls, metal purl and bullion, straw, glass beads, silk cord, linen ribbon, padding. Wood, marbled paper, silver handles. Stitches include French knot, upright gobelin, rococo, eyelet, detached buttonhole and metal work. 280 x 160 x 340 mm (11 x 6.3 x 13.3 in).
There are five panels on this box, and the one illustrated depicts the Jewish biblical heroine Judith, symbolising Humility, holding the severed head of her people's enemy, Holofernes. The unicorn on the right, with his horn raised, symbolises Pride. Thus the entire image represents the way indomitable Pride is overcome through the strength of absolute Humility. (Dorset County Museum 1955.2.9)

22. *(Opposite page)* MIXED BAND SAMPLER. 'Mary Cyttance' (or Cyttange). English School, dated 1676.
Plain weave linen; silk thread, linen thread. Stitches include four-sided, long-armed cross, twisted and back chain, double running, eyelet, satin, stem and cutwork. 466 x 216 mm (18.4 x 8.6 in).
The edges of the prominent hole in this sampler were overcast at an early date to contain the damage. Samplers such as this were intended to teach the novice a variety of patterns and progressively complicated techniques, 'Rare Italian cutworke', as referred to by John Taylor in his poem 'The Prayse of the Needle' (1640), and seen here in the bottom bands, made its appearance on samplers from the 1640s, when the wearing of lace became fashionable. Other examples exhibited show that the two techniques, cutwork and polychrome embroidery, were also learned separately (Nos. 14, 15). (Dorset County Museum T142)

24. FIVE RAISED WORK PANELS. English School, about 1685.
Satin-weave silk, silk lining; silk thread, linen thread, metallic thread, wire, braid, fringing, satin padding, mica, pearls, amber wax. Stitches and techniques include appliqué, tent, moss work, couching, French knot, encroaching gobelin. Top panel, 275 x 369 mm (11 x 14.75 in); front and back, 94 x 369 mm (3.75 x 14.75 in); side panels, 94 x 275 mm (3.25 x 11 in).

These panels were once assembled to complete the sides of a flat-top box. The central panel shows Charles II, identified by the cypher on the open book he is holding, and Catherine of Braganza offering him a small floral tribute, (or a token of pregnancy) attended by an African page and a lady in waiting. The subject matter is dynastic, illustrated by biblical references: Tobias, accompanied by the Angel Raphael, extracting the lights from the fish with which to exorcize demons from his future wife Sara; a betrothal; and the visitation by three angels announcing the birth of a son to the aged Abraham and his wife Sarah. (Dorset County Museum 1984.4.1)

25. NEEDLEWORK LOOKING GLASS BORDER. Partially worked. English School, 1690s.

Satin-weave silk; silk thread; ink. Stitches include satin, cross, stem, and straight. 620 x 520 mm (24.5 x 20.5 in).

The embroiderer has begun her work at the base of the design and the small triangles are experiments with coloured threads. The elaborate outer scroll shape and inner oval were designed to accommodate and aggrandize an expensive steel plate glass. The dense design includes personifications of the Four Seasons, enlivened with flora and fauna and a fish pool with rocks sprouting coral. Illustrated (centre top) is the Judgement of Paris, here in shepherd guise offering the golden apple to Venus. Minerva and Juno, the losers, are relegated as side suppporters. (Royal School of Needlework)

26. BAND SAMPLER. English School, 1690s.
Plain weave linen; Tussah silk thread, silver-gilt thread, sheep's tow padding. Stitches include cross, long armed cross, eyelet, stem, gobelin, plaited braid and detached buttonhole. Selvedge at the top. 395 x 225 mm (15.5 x 8 in).

This sampler shares many elements in common with the work of Alice and Margaret Jennings, whose samplers are dated 1692 and 1695 respectively (Dr Goodhart Collection, Montacute House, National Trust). Each of the three is structured so that a line of text alternates with a band of pattern. The second and bottom polychrome bands are common to all three pieces. These, and other similarities, suggest that all were worked under the direction of an unidentified teacher, or that each had access to the same pattern book source. (Siva Swaminathan Collection)

27. BAND SAMPLER WITH FIGURES. English School, late seventeenth century.
Plain weave linen; single and double strands of silk thread. Stitches include cross, upright gobelin, Florentine, stem, outline, double-running, speckling and knitting. 388 x 190 mm (15.5 x 7 in).

The freedom with which the human figures in the centre band have been delineated contrasts strikingly with the formality of the band patterns. The needleworker may have deliberately chosen to defy current convention, or possibly the figurative motifs are a later intervention, as the female figure is awkwardly placed in the design field. The relative position of the figures is reminiscent of a Johannes Sibmacher whitework pattern. (Siva Swaminathan Collection)

NO PARTICULAR RULE FOR THE STITCHER
1715–1797

The old style band sampler which dominated the seventeenth century persisted for a time into the eighteenth. Gradually, however, the horizontal patterns were modified for use as horizontal and vertical borders, sometimes with mitred pattern corners. These patterns also broke free of their stiffness and were transformed into more naturalistic forms. Spot motifs that had their origins in Dutch embroidery were combined with borders and band patterns in symmetrical arrangements on the ground fabric. With enclosed sayings and verses, the sampler became a decorative object in its own right. As one amused eighteenth century observer recorded, 'Miss is set down to her frame before she can put on her clothes, and is taught to believe that to excel at her needle is the only thing that can entitle her to general esteem.' In rural Dorset, young fingers were busy with their samplers. Martha Sampson worked hers at Yetminster School, the first of three from the same village school (Nos. 39, 51, 52).

Young embroiderers no longer raised figure families on hipped caskets, which themselves carried faint echoes of dolls' houses. Older and now married mistresses of more substantial houses, the legacy of the Georgian building boom, they covered their furniture with Arcadian pastoral, classical and mythological narrative canvas work (Nos. 29, 32). By the middle of the eighteenth century the phrases 'to flower' and 'to embroider' were synonymous. By the 1760s, ornamentation on waistcoats and dresses (Nos. 32, 38), responding to the design influences from imported Indian cottons, trailed with naturalistic flowers, reflecting the new decorative sampler borders. 'Foliage, fruits, flowers and drapery is all they need to know to create their own embroidery pattern if they can't find one that suits them,' wrote J. J. Rousseau in *Emile* in 1762.

Free-style silk pictures commemorated dead heroes or lovers, and needleworkers made woollen portraits of the famous (No. 37). Twenty years after Captain Cook's Antipodean voyages, meticulously charted embroidered maps on silk (No. 45) recorded the new discoveries. Even the upheavals of the French Revolution are hinted at in a fervent if phlegmatic 'Long Live The King and Queen' (No. 40).

28. INSCRIBED DROP POCKET. English School, about 1715.
Ecru silk with cyclamen silk lining. Cross stitch. The lining was unravelled to form the fringe. Horizontal opening slit. 230 x 260 mm (9.25 x 10.5 in)
The pattern on this elegant pocket was influenced by contemporary sampler motifs. The two verse inscription suggests that just as a tear-shaped drop pocket hangs, so life itself hangs suspended from the flimsiest of threads. (Royal School of Needlework).

'Good God on what slender thread
Hang everlasting things
The eternal state of all things dead
Upon life's feeble strings.

Infinite joy or endless woe
Attend on every breath
And yet how unconcerned we go
Upon the brink of death.'

29. CHAIR SEAT COVER. Partially worked. English School, 1720-30.
Linen canvas; worsted wool yarn. Stitches and techniques include applied work and tent. A coarser linen piece, also partly worked, has been attached but not applied. 570 x 550 mm (22.5 x 21.75 in). Canvas with slips for applying: 95 x 150 mm (3.75 x 5.25 in).

Embroidered rural scenes, expressing a fashionable predilection for the Arcadian or rustic pastoral life, became popular for use on articles of furniture during the first decades of the eighteenth century. They evolved from canvaswork compositions from the two previous centuries (No. 10), when their subject matter had been drawn from biblical and classical sources. In the 1700s biblical subjects fell from favour while classical narrative pictorials remained popular. The canvaswork slip details of the man's face and hands have been applied to the ground canvas and padded. The stitched details of the woman's image remain unfinished. A faint inscription in the right-hand corner of the canvas reads 'Mary'. (Embroiderers' Guild Collection EG3428)

Cat. No. 29 © Embroiderers' Guild
Photographer: Julia Hedgecoe

30. MINIATURE ALPHABET SAMPLER. English School, 1733.
Plain weave linen; silk thread. Stitches include running, cross, and braid. 115 x 97 mm (4.75 x 4.5 in).

The sampler is inscribed with 'PSALM 92' and 'SS HER/WORK IN THE 9 OF HER AGE 1733', with numerals as line fillers. Space has not been left between the words, as was quite common at this date, as the priority was to complete the stitchery; comprehension came a poor second. A later hand-written note appended to the back of the mount states: 'On this sampler (Sarah Shippard's) the 92 Psalm'. Followed by an inaccurate rendering of the embroidered text. (Siva Swaminathan Collection)

31. RANDOM SAMPLER. 'Elizabeth Spear 1734/35'. English School.
Two lengths of plain weave linen, joined by a French seam at 444 mm (17.75 in) from the top edge; silk thread, silver-gilt and other metal threads. Stitches include buttonhole, chain, twisted chain, cross, star cross, long and short, satin, stem, single faggot, split, Algerian eye, French knot, double-running, Greek, and fly. Approx. 1080 x 245 mm (43 x 9.5 in).

Inscribed with alphabets, initials and two dates. Rare for samplers of this date, the selvedges are along the two long edges rather than at the top and bottom. In upper case lettering is an abbreviated Lord's Prayer and identification of a few of the motifs: 'THIS IS THE OLIVE TREE/THE CHERRY TREE/THIS IS A DOUBLE FRENCH MERRY GOVLD.' The style of this sampler is distinctive and original, with strikingly individualistic spot motifs, including the biblical image of Solomon's Porch. (Dorset County Museum 1950.7.1.)

32. FLORAL BORDER. English School, 1740s.
Silk gound; silk thread, silver-gilt metal thread. Stitches include long and short, satin, and stem. Techniques include couching. *975 x 425 mm (39 x 17 in).*
Embroidered borders such as this were used to decorate women's petticoats, which were worn underneath a robe. The needlework would have been visible under the inverted V-shaped gap in the skirt of an 'open' robe. Versions of this kind of border can be found on formal aprons, where the designs extend up the sides. The treatment of the leaves, with their metallic shading, is as important as the colouring of the flowers, a style echoed in crewel work embroidery. (Siva Swaminathan Collection)

34. SPOT MOTIF SAMPLER. Mary Sime. Scottish School, 1768.
Plain weave tammy (worsted yarn); silk thread. Worked almost entirely in cross and back stitch. 253 x 324 mm (10 x 13 in).
The maker's name is worked modestly in small lettering and the larger three sets of initials may be those of her parents, along with her own. The curlicue letter type, characteristic of Scottish samplers, originated in the Netherlands. The band pattern at the bottom, a favourite amongst seventeenth century sample makers, is similar to one on a Scottish sampler of 1762 illustrated in Marcus Huish *Samplers*. Its inclusion on this sampler reinforces the view that patterns were used over long periods by needleworkers living in remote areas and with little access to new designs. However, the tammy ground, with a blue thread woven in its selvedges, would have been purchased from a draper or pedlar. (Dorset County Museum 1953-17-3)

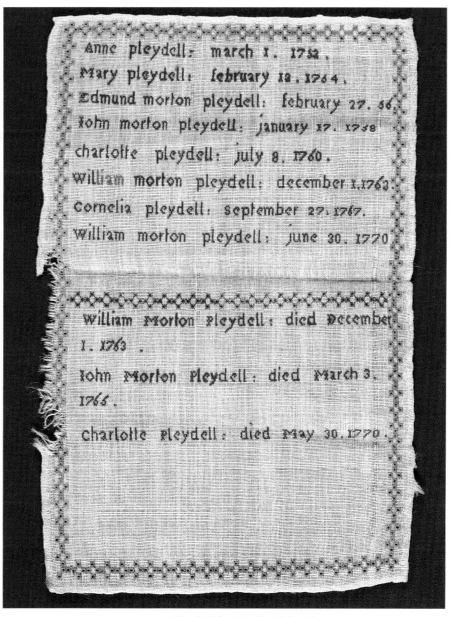

35. GENEALOGICAL SAMPLER. Pleydell family. English, after 1770.
Plain weave tammy; silk thread. Cross stitch. 230 x 148 mm (9.1 x 5.7 in).
Tamine or tammy cloth, from the French *'étamine'*, a sieve, was widely available. This unadorned sampler is inscribed with the names and dates of birth of eight children, born between 1752 and 1770, to Edmund and Anne Pleydell, of Milborne St Andrew, Dorset. The lower half marks the deaths of three of them, with space left for additional names. The date and identity of the (Pleydell)? needleworker remains unknown. For more information on the Pleydell family and the background to this sampler see the Introduction, page 9. (Dorset County Museum 1978.16.)

36. DECORATIVE PANEL. English, 1770.

Thirteen plain weave linen panels pieced together with flat seams; silk thread.
Stitches include outline, Florentine, stem, satin, French knot, tent, cross, buttonhole,
and long and short. 610 x 765 mm (24 x 30 in).

Inscribed: 'Mary Portar Sampler Wrought In The 14 Year of Her Age In The Year of
Our Lord 1770 Youngest Daughter of John and Mary Portar of Northsomercoates'.

In this sampler, the youngest daughter of the Portar family learned and
demonstrated mastery of three decorative skills: floral, Florentine and lettering. This
is an elegant, well-planned design, skilfully worked. The flame-like Florentine
patterns were used for furniture upholstery and to embellish both personal and
ecclesiastical vestments. The flowers in the lightly meandering border later became
fashionable for the decoration of dress. (Siva Swaminathan Collection)

37. NEEDLE PAINTING PANEL. Signed and dated, 'M K 1779'. English.
Hand-woven plain weave tammy; wool yarn. Stitches include satin, and random long and short. 892 x 845 mm (35.5 x 33.5 in).

The panel depicts Mary Morris Knowles embroidering a copy of Zoffany's portrait of George III. Best remembered for her needle painting, the Quaker Mary Knowles was introduced to Queen Charlotte by the Royal Academician Benjamin West. At that time women were not encouraged to join the Academy Schools and as an alternative developed the art of needle painting in order to pursue their interest in portraiture. Queen Charlotte commissioned Knowles to make a needlework copy of Johann Zoffany's recent portrait of the King.

Horace Walpole in the *Anecdotes of Painting* (1762) commented: 'This art of copying in work by the eye, with no particular rule for the stitches, was invented by Miss Grey, daughter of a clergyman.' (Lent by Her Majesty The Queen RCIN/11912)

38. EMBROIDERED WAISTCOAT. Detail of pocket. English, about 1780.
Satin-weave silk ground for front, twill weave silk and brushed cotton for back, silk lining, silk-covered buttons; silk floss. Stitches include satin, straight. Centre back: 675 x chest 900 mm (27 x 36 in).
Amy Garland embroidered this waistcoat for her husband George. The field of the front of the waistcoat is strewn with flowers and diagonal rows of zig-zags alternating with green spots. Remarkably, we know who worked this waistcoat, for whom, and what both of them looked like. The Museum collection includes a pair of pendant portraits of Mr and Mrs George Garland by an unknown painter. (Dorset County Museum 1978.10.1.)

39. ALPHABET BAND SAMPLER. 'Martha Sampson'. English School, 1787.
Plain weave linen; silk thread. Stitches and techniques include pulled thread, Algerian eye, eyelet, long-armed cross, and cross. 420 x 198 mm (16.6 x 7.9 in).

The sampler reads like a page from a school primer. A simple border pattern encloses horizontal bands of alphabets and numerals. Inscribed 'Martha Sampson,/ Yetminster School,/ October 18th 1787'. 'The politeness of the mind lies / in . . . virtuous and delicate / reflections.' Above various bands are appropriate headings, such as 'THE ALPHABET', 'Small Letters' and 'FIGURES'.

Two other samplers from Yetminster School, Dorset, are also illustrated in this catalogue (Nos. 51, 52), and a fourth is known to exist. There have been many schools in the village of Yetminster, and the site of the one referred to in these embroideries is no longer known, though it was probabaly a 'dame' school in a private house. (Dorset County Museum 1917-8-3)

40. SAMPLER. 'Elizabeth Kirk'. English, 1789.
Plain weave linen; silk thread. Stitches include satin, cross, French knot, and stem.
600 x 455 mm (23.75 x 17.75 in).
Elizabeth worked two bordered fields in her sampler. The first is inscribed
'ELIZABETH KIRK WORK'D THIS. MAY 1789 IN THE NINTH YEAR OF HER AGE. LINCOLN',
followed by three texts. The recording of a place name on an English sampler at this
date is uncommon. The other enclosure, filled with spot motifs, is inscribed 'Long
Live The King and Queen'. Dated two months before the Fall of the Bastille,
Elizabeth Kirk appears to have been staunchly Royalist. (Siva Swaminathan
Collection)

41. SILK PICTURE. English School, late 1790s.

Satin weave silk; silk thread, silk chenille thread, water colour. Stitches include long and short, stem, and French knot. 290 x 240 mm (11.25 x 9.25 in).

The painted details of the background depict three men and two women indulging in the pagan pleasure of dancing round the maypole, protected by its proximity to the church. In the foreground a young woman, supported by a friend and her companion, swoons with pleasure as a young swain invites her to dance with him and the traditional May Day revellers. (Private Collection)

[45]

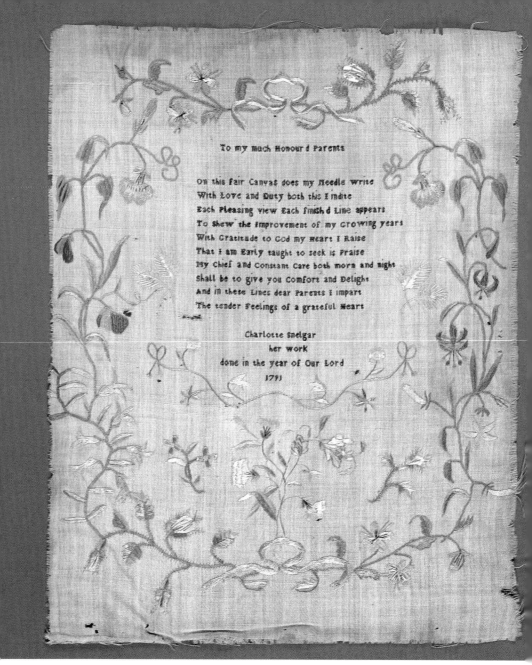

To my much Honour'd Parents

On this fair Canvas does my Needle write
With Love and Duty both this I indite
Each Pleasing view Each finish'd Line appears
To Shew the Improvement of my Growing years
With Gratitude to God my Heart I Raise
That I am Early taught to seek is Praise
My Chief and Constant Care both morn and night
Shall be to give you Comfort and Delight
And in these Lines dear Parents I impart
The tender Feelings of a grateful Heart

Charlotte Snelgar
her work
done in the year of Our Lord
1791

42. SAMPLER. 'Charlotte Snelgar'. English School, 1791.
Plain weave wool; silk thread. Stitches include cross, stem, satin, open chain, and variations. 420 x 334 mm (16.6 x 13.25 in).
Enclosed within the delicate floriated and beribboned border is a dedication 'To my much Honour'd parents' and a ten-line filial tribute in couplets, worked in fine black lettering, beginning, 'On this fair Canvas does my needle write', and ending with her own name: ' Charlotte Snelgar/her work/done in the year of Our Lord/1791'. (Dorset County Museum 1972.43)

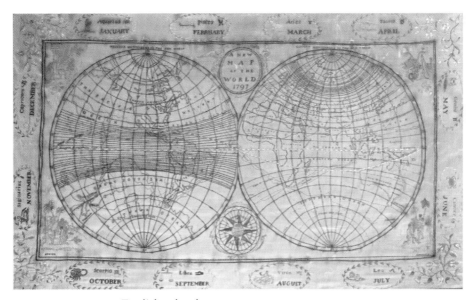

43. MAP SAMPLER. English school, 1797.
Satin-weave silk; silk thread. Stitches include back, outline, and satin. 490 x 825 mm (19.5 x 32.25 in).
Entitled 'A NEW MAP OF THE WORLD', and charting Cook's voyages to the Antipodes. The island of Tasmania is shown joined to the Australian mainland. Twenty years after the discovery of Australia the notion that there were more than four continents had still to gain acceptance, with the result that idealized renderings of the 'peoples' of Europe, Asia, America and Africa have been placed in the four corners. The borders include inscribed Signs of the Zodiac and the Months of the Year.

A similar map-panel is inscribed 'For Ladies Needlework and Young Students in Geography', perhaps belying the view that the needlework maps were designed exclusively as schoolroom exercises. (Siva Swaminathan Collection)

[47]

HER FINGERS ON THE SAMPLER MOVE
1801– 1890

Nineteenth century sampler designs were interpreted in either free style embroidery (Nos. 55, 63) or in the more limited cross stitch, which produces geometric-looking motifs. The latter, strongly influenced by the Dutch style, can be seen in the 'Tree of Life', fruit baskets and birds. (Nos. 46, 56, 58, 64).

A comparison between the three samplers from Yetminster shows how radically the basic design format changed between 1787 and 1821 (Nos 39, 51, 52). Two samplers represent monochrome work, Rebecca Benwell's from Milverton School in Somerset, testifying to the virtue of Quaker perseverance, and an anonymous Bristol Orphanage sampler (Nos. 44, 84). An elegant, skilful darning piece reverts to the original intention of the sampler, demonstrating how a plain sewing technique can be transformed into an object of beauty (No. 45).

The fundamentalist moral tone of the previous period continued in the 1800s. Churches, Sunday Schools and the 'All-Seeing' eye of God appear as reminders that 'Religion should our thoughts Engage/Amidst our Youthful bloom' (No. 64). In contrast, some samplers depict elegant town houses or prosperous farms, their fields filled with livestock (No. 53). Esther Stewart's sampler (No. 61) is more politically aware than the other embroideries illustrated for this period, and was worked to draw attention to the evils of slavery. Further research should reveal which designs and techniques were favoured by the different social classes that formed the rigid Victorian class structure.

'When a house is said to be furnished it conveys the idea of it being fitted up with every necessity, both useful and ornamental'. So wrote the furniture maker Thomas Sheraton in 1803. This philosophy was taken to heart by the emerging Victorian middle-class. From the middle of the nineteenth century, helped by the invention of aniline dyes and aided by hand-coloured pictorial charts, needleworkers covered small furnishings and panels (Nos. 69, 64) in omnipresent Berlin woolwork, using patterns first worked on long and narrow Berlin woolwork samplers (No. 67).

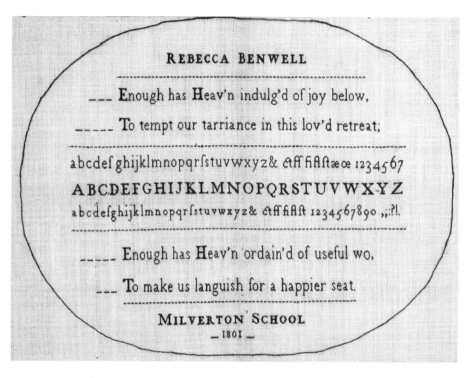

REBECCA BENWELL

___ Enough has Heav'n indulg'd of joy below,

_____ To tempt our tarriance in this lov'd retreat;

abcdefghijklmnopqrſstuvwxyz& ctff fiflſtæœ 1234567

ABCDEFGHIJKLMNOPQRSTUVWXYZ

abcdefghijklmnopqrſstuvwxyz& ctff fiflſt 1234567890 ,,:?!.

_____ Enough has Heav'n ordain'd of useful wo,

___ To make us languish for a happier seat.

MILVERTON SCHOOL
_ 1801 _

44. SAMPLER. 'Rebecca Benwell'. English, 1801.
Plain weave linen; silk thread. Cross stitch. 280 x 210 mm (11 x 8.5 in).
Rebecca Benwell was born in 1787, the daughter of Quakers, John and Martha Benwell. Milverton School was privately run at the Friends House in Milverton, Somerset, by Sarah Young. 'A Map of England and Wales' sampler, of 1806, was worked by another pupil at the school, Hannah Burge. Both show diligent application and fine attention to detail, and were probably created under the tutelage of Sarah Young. (Siva Swaminathan Collection)

45. DARNING SAMPLER. 'Mary Ann Ranson'. English School, 1802.
Gauze weave cotton; silk thread. Stitches include cross, long and short, stem, and French knot. The pattern darning samples illustrate the following weaves; twill, herringbone, diamond damask, and double diamond damask. 365 x 430 mm (14 x 17 in).
While the pattern darning in this sampler looks both delicate and decorative, its practical purpose as a plain sewing technique was to repair damage to napery and the high-waisted muslin dresses of the Regency. The darning sampler form retains the last vestiges of the original purpose of the sampler, a repository and learning piece for patterns and techniques. The initials 'F.R', worked in ecru thread at the base of the work, make modest reference to the tutor, perhaps related to Mary Ann Ranson. (Siva Swaminathan Collection)

46. *(Opposite page)* SAMPLER. 'Clementina Reddrop'. English School, 1804.
Plain weave linen; silk thread. Cross stitch. 490 x 325 mm (19.5 x 12 in).
Two men bear the weight of an outsized bunch of grapes as witness to the fecundity of the Promised Land: this was a well-established bibical image in the stories of Moses. Inscribed, 'These are the Spies which went to view the land of Canaan', and 'the Lord reigneth in Zion', with the initials 'CR'. As with the Adam and Eve motif, the image fulfilled a double purpose in embroidery, it was both instructive and symmetrical. (Siva Swaminathan Collection)

Children — are defirous, and expect that God
fhould protect and blefs them, muft dutifully obey
their Parents, and follow the good Precepts of their
Teachers and Guardians.

MARY BRADLEY AGED 11 YEARS LEI
GH SCHOOL FEBRUARY 24th 1804

47. PICTORIAL SAMPLER. 'Mary Bradley'. English, 1804.
Plain weave wool; silk thread. Stitches include cross, satin, and straight. 318 x 275 mm (12.75 x 11 in).
Inscribed: 'MARY BRADLEY AGED 11 YEARS LEI/GH SCHOOL FEBRUARY 14TH 1804'.
There is probably some connection between this and another sampler (No. 50) marked 'Ann Bradley, 18 October 1811'. Both show a building that may well have been Leigh School, and there is much that is similar in the design and format of the two samplers. The two girls may have been sisters or cousins, and were perhaps taught by the same teacher. (Dorset County Museum 1972-49-1)

48. SAMPLER MOTIF HOLDER WITH POCKETS.

Shown open and closed.

English, 1805-1815.

Linen buckram, net, silk ribbon, silk thread. Cross stitch. 213 x 85 mm (8.5 x 3.5 in).

Both sides of the holder are decorated with sampler motifs, including the Tree of Life. A stitched inscription begins, 'O Lord my God in mercy turn/In mercy hear a sinner mourn'. This is a nice combination of a practice piece with a practical secondary application. Designed to be hung and hold small sewing items, the motifs on the top third section are not worked in a reverse position, as would have been the case with a purse. (Private Collection)

ABCDEFG H I K M OPQRSTUV XYZ
23 56 89

Accept dear Lord an Infants Prayer
And make my future Life thy care
Be thou my Guardian Father Friend
Support and Guide me to the end
Preserve from sins destructive ways
And teach my Tongue to lisp thy Praise
To act the wise and better Part
And serve the Lord with all my heart
Make me Industrious virtuous good
And wash my soul in Jesus Blood
Then if Distrest or poor or of s
My portion be I'll bear the Cross
Upheld by thee I never can fall
For Jesus is my all in all ——

Mary Champs   Work 1809

49. PICTORIAL SAMPLER. 'Mary Champ'. English School, 1809.
Plain weave tammy; silk thread, wool yarn. Cross stitch. Two selvedges on the left and right sides. 312 x 325 mm (12.25 x 12.75 in).
The focal point of this elegant sampler is a red-brick three-storied town house with prominent territorial railings. The dispersed spot motifs, arranged symmetrically, are evidence of northern European pattern influences originating in the Low Countries. The motifs begin to appear with regularity from about 1700. (Dorset County Museum 1950.7.3.)

50. DECORATIVE SAMPLER. 'Ann Bradley'. English, dated October 18 1811.
Plain weave tammy; silk thread. Cross stitch. 340 x 300 mm (13.5 x 11.75 in).
Inscribed: 'Honour thy Father with thy whole heart and forget not the kindness of
thy Mother, how canst thou recompense them the things they have done for thee.'
The two-storied vernacular building is similar to the one depicted in the Mary
Bradley sampler (No. 47). It is probable that the girls were sisters, or otherwise
related. (J.K. Wingfield-Digby Esq.,)

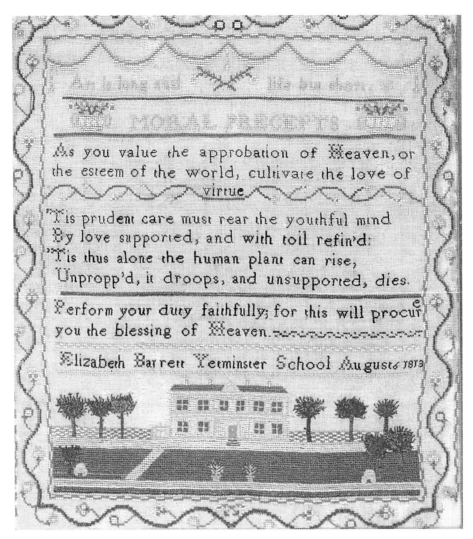

51. YETMINSTER SCHOOL SAMPLER. 'Elizabeth Barrett'. English, 1813.
Plain weave tammy; silk thread. Cross stitch. 288 x 256 mm (11.5 x 10.25 in).
The school is depicted bordered by six pollarded trees. Inscribed, 'Art is long and life but short', followed by a succession of 'Moral Precepts': 'As you value the approbation of Heaven, or the esteem of the world cultivate the love of virtue.' 'Tis prudent care must rear the youthful mind / By Love supported and with toil refin'd / 'Tis thus alone the human plant can rise / Unpropped it droops and unsupported dies' with 'Perform your duty faithfully, for this will procure you the blessing of Heaven'. Note the raised 'e' on 'procure' where Eizabeth Barrett had run out of space at the end of the line. The sampler hangs in a corridor at the present school in the village. (St Andrew's V.C. Primary School, Yetminster, Dorset)

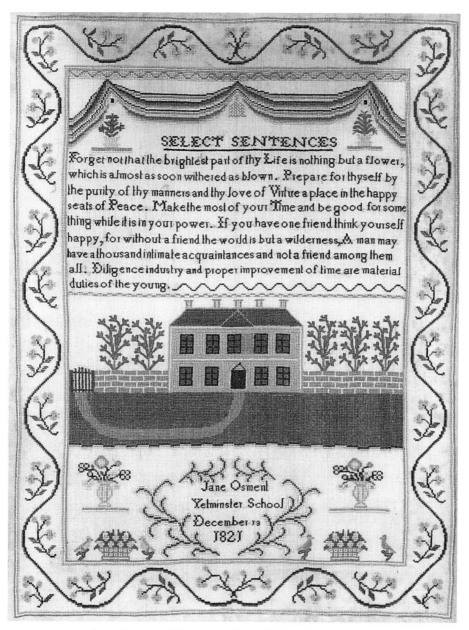

The sampler text reads:

SELECT SENTENCES

Forget not that the brightest part of thy Life is nothing but a flower, which is almost as soon withered as blown. Prepare for thyself by the purity of thy manners and thy love of Virtue a place in the happy seats of Peace. Make the most of your Time and be good for some thing while it is in your power. If you have one friend think yourself happy, for without a friend the world is but a wilderness, A man may have a thousand intimate acquaintances and not a friend among them all. Diligence industry and proper improvement of time are material duties of the young.

Jane Osment
Yetminster School
December 13
1821

52 . SAMPLER. 'Jane Osment, Yetminster School'. English, 1821.
Plain weave tammy; silk thread. Cross stitch. 538 x 438 mm (21.5 x 17.25 in).
The design field is disposed in a format similar to Elizabeth Barrett's sampler on the opposite page. Both were pupils at the same school, but eight years have elapsed and one of the six trees is no longer standing. A fourth sampler from the same school is known. Note how the heading 'Moral Precepts' of the previous sampler has now become 'Select Sentences'. (Witney Antiques)

53. SPOT MOTIF SAMPLER. 'Elizabeth Smith'. English School, 1814.
Plain weave linen; silk thread. Stitches include cross, and French knot. 690 x 470 mm (27 x 18.5 in).

In this embroidery, the border has become less significant, giving way to an enlarged pictorial field, powdered with incident. The upper register of the sampler features a six-verse religious inscription, beginning with, 'Christ dwells in Heaven but visits on earth' (Canticles) fills the upper register. Using a variety of motifs, Elizabeth Smith has recorded boats, buildings, and flora and fauna in the form of farm stock, including a favoured horse. Two motifs enclosed in garlands, are inscribed with Elizabeth Smith's name, age and the year. (Siva Swaminathan Collection)

54. PICTORIAL SAMPLER. 'Mary Drake'. English School, 1815.

Plain weave linen; silk floss. Stitches include chain, stem, cross, and satin. Selvedges, left and right. 448 x 340 mm. (17.25 x 13.5 in).

Inscribed: 'Mary Drake Aetas [aged] 12 Years 1815' with two moral texts. The sampler has a lightness of touch and an unforced symmetry, with a lightly meandering border. Having only recently been made aware of their nakedness, Adam and Eve have sewn fig leaves together and made themselves aprons. (Dorset County Museum 1962.30)

ABCDEFGHIJKLMNOPQRSTUVWXYZ&12

abcdefghiklmnopqrstuvwxyz&1234567891011121314151617181920 21

Character of Christ.
Behold, where, in a mortal form,
Appears each grace divine,
The virtues, all in Jesus meet,
With mildest radiance shine.

Lowly in heart, by all his friends,
A friend and servant found;
He wash'd their feet, he wip'd their tears
And heal'd each bleeding wound.

Be Christ my pattern and my guide,
His image may I bear,
O may I tread his sacred steps,
And his bright glories share.

Ann Garness   June 16 1820

55. (*Opposite page*) SAMPLER. 'Ann Garness'. English School, 1820/6.
Plain weave linen; silk thread. Stitches include cross, stem, cross, satin, and French knot. 525 x 325 mm (21 x 13 in).
Several design traditions are conjoined in this sampler. Repeating bands in the form of an arcaded honeysuckle border and a carnation pattern echo embroidered bands of the seventeenth century. The pair of baskets, from the northern European tradition, are incorporated into a naturalistic design with an exotic Australian cockatoo perching on a fruiting branch. A more modern touch, roses set into vases, support a text entitled the 'Character of Christ.' The original embroidered date of 1820 has been altered in ink, and put forward by six years, almost certainly to conceal the maker's age. (Siva Swaminathan Collection)

56. SAMPLER. 'Elizabeth Wightman'. English School, 1827.
Plain weave linen; silk thread. Stitches include cross, and satin. 363 x 333 mm (14.25 x 13.25 in).
Inscribed: 'Elizabeth Wightman's work Aged 11 Years February 1827', with a popular pious poem.
   Designed with a sparse formality, with an enlarged arcaded border, this sampler has been skillfully embroidered. The back is as presentable as the front, and no connecting threads are visible. (Dorset County Museum 1942-24-1)

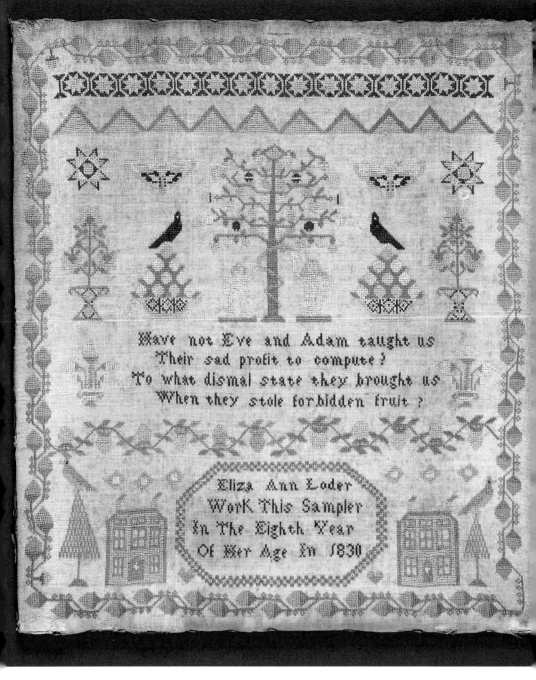

Have not Eve and Adam taught us
Their sad profit to compute?
To what dismal state they brought us
When they stole forbidden fruit?

Eliza Ann Loder
Work This Sampler
In The Eighth Year
Of Her Age In 1830

58. PICTORIAL SAMPLER. 'Eliza Ann Loder'. English School, 1830.
Plain weave tammy, linen lining; silk thread. Cross stitch. Selvedges are at the left and right edges. 372 x 335 mm (14.75 x 13.75 in).
This is a favourite sampler motif. Adam and Eve stand by the multi-coloured fruit 'Tree of Knowledge', depicted espaliered in the French fashion, and around which the serpent winds sinuously as Eve reaches up to the forbidden fruit. All the other spot motifs are placed with a fine eye to symmetry. (Dorset County Museum 1941.11)

61. SAMPLER. 'Esther Stewart'. English School, 1836.
Plain weave tammy; silk thread, wool yarn. Cross stitch. 510 x 520 mm (20 x 20.5 in).
Inscribed '1836 Esther Stewart her work. The African Slave'.

Worked two years before the Abolition of Slavery Bill was finally enacted, this recording of a social injustice is rare in needlework. Anna Sebba in *Samplers* records the same image worked by Susan Bradshaw in 1853. The chained slave pleads to the Lord for mercy. The line of sheep at his feet symbolize the need that both Man and sheep have of the Good Shepherd. (Witney Antiques)

62. SPOT SAMPLER. 'Lucy Palmar'. English School, 1837.
Plain weave tammy; cotton thread. Stitches include Algerian eye, eyelet, and cross.
355 x 305 mm (14 x 12 in).
An unpunctuated inscription reads:

    'Give to the Father praise
    Give Glory to the Son
    And to the spirit of His Grace
    Be eternal honour done'

  A second alphabet row was begun and abandoned after the letter 'B', and the twenty-two-year-old Lucy obviously had difficulty with the spelling of 'February'. Much of the pictorial needlework has been executed skillfully. Lucy Palmar worked her surname in almost invisible ecru thread in mirror writing. (Miss Pamela Froud)

63. FLOREATE PANEL. 'Sarah Wooldridge'. English School, 1842.
Plain weave linen of approximately 48 threads per inch; twisted silk. Stitches include long and short, outline, French knot, couching, steam, and cross.
Although she had trouble with spacing, and aligning the corners, Sarah Wooldridge's work is ambitious and technically accomplished, especially for a ten-year-old! Inscribed:

> The morning Flowers display their sweets
> As careless of the noontide heats
> As fearless of the evening cold
> Nipt by the winds unkindly blast,
> Parch'd by the sun's directer ray
> The mometary glories waste
> The short-lived beauties die away.

The exuberant design - and the survival of the needlework itself - contradicts the pessimism of the verse. (Siva Swaminathan Collection)

64. DECORATIVE PANEL. 'Margaret Winkley'. English School, 1840s.
Plain weave linen; silk thread; wool yarn. Stitches include turkey work, cross, stem, satin, French knot, and outline. 663 x 550 mm (26.5 x 22 in).
A leafy street scene with an imposing church, a Sunday School, farm animals and a beehive alive with symbolic busy bees. Enclosed in a meandering floral border with birds and butterflies, the panel is distinguished by the unusual design of an 'All-Seeing' eye bathed in celestial light supported by a cherub and a seraph. Inscribed at the bottom, 'Margaret Winkley Aged 9 Years'. (Siva Swaminathan Collection)

65. DECORATIVE PANEL. English School, 1855-65.

Linen canvas of approximately 30 threads per inch; chenille wool yarn; glass beads. Stitches include cross and plush. Berlin wool work technique. Circular mount diameter 350 mm (14 in).

Plush stitch, also known as astrakhan and velvet stitch, is an early technique which imitates the woven pile of Oriental carpets and gives a third dimension to the needlework. Its use was revived during the Victorian period, between 1850 and 1870. Worked as a counted thread looped stitch with a cross stitch attachment. It can be left as a loop; however, a trimming tool was required to create a pile of uniform length.

The designer of this pattern is unkown, but the style closely resembles the work of Louis Gluer. (Private Collection)

66. SPOT SAMPLER. 'Mary J'. English School, 1851.
Plain weave linen; cotton thread. Cross stitch. One selvedge. 311 x 419 mm (12.25 x 16.5 in).
Inscribed, 'Mary J Her Work in The 10 Year of Her age 1851'.

   Symmetrical and confident, the effect on the design of the spot motifs in larger scale is simplified. This produces an angular, grid-like effect, with no shading. This sampler was probably worked in a dame school, as the use of the initial 'J' distinguished Mary from the other Marys in the school. (Dorset County Museum T128)

67. BERLIN WOOL WORK SAMPLER. English, 1850s.
Woollen double canvas (Penelope); wool yarn. Stitches include cross and Florentine.
230 x 870 mm (9.25 x 34.5 in).
The use of the sampler returned to its first purpose during the craze for Berlin wool work patterns – that of being a repository of stitches and patterns. Those recorded are almost always small geometric repeats, and Florentine patterns, with only the occasional small spot motif. The wool yarn in this sampler was dyed with aniline dyes, which had been introduced in the 1840s. (Royal School of Needlework)

68. IRISH CHANCELLOR'S BURSE. English School, 1847/1853 or 1859.
Velvet silk pile; silk thread, silver-gilt thread, copper wrapped metallic thread, spangles, braid, padding. Stitches include satin, bullion, French knot, and couching. 520 x 470 mm (20.5 x 18.5 in).

This burse is an example of a professional broderer's work, using ancient techniques in a format that has changed only in detail since the time of Queen Elizabeth I. An insignia of office, it was made for the Irish Chancellor, Sir Mazière Brady (1796-1871). The three dates listed above record his appointment to the Office on three occasions; and traditional practice suggests a burse was made for each of these. The addition of the harp and shamrock in raised cartouches emphasises its Irish provenance. The embroidery can be compared to a burse for the Great Seal made for Francis North in 1682 in the Burrell Collection, Glasgow. (Private Collection)

69. BEADED POT COVER. English School, 1865-75.
Double canvas (Penelope), cotton lining; cotton thread, Saxony wool yarn, glass beads, cotton cord. 230 x 320 x 190 mm (9 x 12.5 x 8 in).
A cheering and amusing rendering of a fashionable tea-pot, milk jug and a cup and saucer. 'Fancy' work and beading overtook the British embroiderer in the mid-nineteenth century. Victorian beads were larger than those in use on Stuart embroidery, and by the 1850s they were everywhere, on purses, tea-pot stands and covers, banners and slippers. (Private Collection)

71. SAMPLER. 'Louisa Cutler'. English, 1860s.
Plain weave tammy, linen backing, paper, pine plank; cotton thread. Cross stitch. 428 x 334 mm (17 x 13.25 in).
Inscribed, 'Louisa Cutler Dewlish School'. In the 1840s type-faces increased in number and variety, with the changes reflected here. The subtle use of shading to enliven the Gothic and Roman scripts lifts this practical marking sampler into something more decorative. (Dorset County Museum T913)

84. BRISTOL ORPHANAGE MARKING SAMPLER. 'M.A. Wrighton'. English, 1878. *Plain weave cotton; cotton thread. Cross stitch. 375 x 290 mm (15 x 11.3 in).*
The marking of household and personal linen was learned by doing a marking sampler. Letters of various styles and patterns were embroidered in marking or cross stitch by counting the threads of the ground fabric. The usual thread colours were blue and red. The Bristol Orphanages were founded in 1829, and taught plain sewing and knitting to children of both sexes. The inclusion of 'Home Sweet Home' in this context carries a certain poignancy. (Siva Swaminathan Collection)

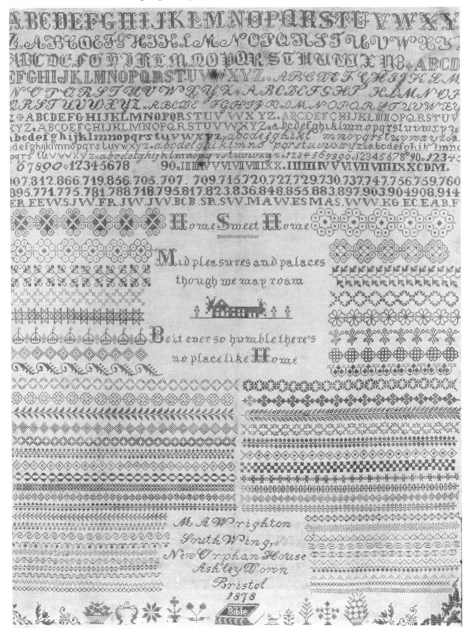

85. INSCRIBED HAIR SAMPLER. 'Annie Parker'. English School, 1880s.
Plain weave linen; human hair, silk thread. Stitches include feather, double feather,
cross; crochet work. 510 x 410 mm (20.25 x 16.25 in).
Human hair had been used in the late eighteenth century to embroider landscapes
that imitated Dutch engravings.

Annie Parker (1850-1885) was an alcoholic, and frequently imprisoned by the
authorities. Her four-verse inscription, with the reprise 'Thy will be done', begins
'My God my Father while I stray / Far from my home in life's rough way'. Blank
dedicatory space is left below.

A sampler with a similar devout inscription dated 'June '82', was worked and
presented by her to the Governor of Bedford Prison's daughter. A hair work
pincushion by her is in the Black Museum at New Scotland Yard. (Witney Antiques)

GLORIOUS NEEDLEPOINT
1902 – 2000

The twentieth century saw an extraordinary diversity in embroidery. While no evident dominating style emerged, the new trend was towards the decorative in preference to the practical. This was coupled by an interest in using newly discovered materials and the new techniques of collage and machine embroidery. Commercial interests influenced designs by promoting transfer patterns and stamped embroidery kits (No. 86).

The design of twentieth-century embroidery was sometimes retrospective and nostalgic. In an effort to expand a depleted repertoire, attempts were made to restore lost patterns. Established historical techniques were revived, particularly raised embroidery, the three dimensional padded figurative work popular during the Stuart period. Using historic stitches, the parameters of raised work were extended with the use of new man-made materials, including PVC glue, which has its own historical precedent in the potato starch originally used to adhere applied canvaswork slips on to a ground.

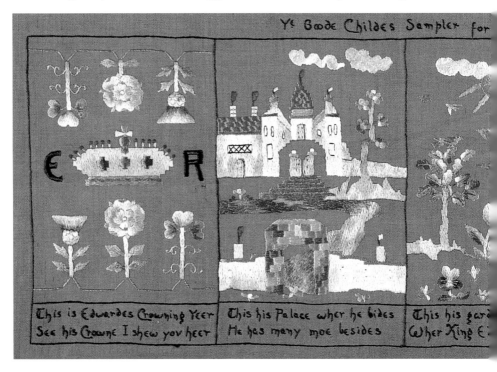

But a new ethic prevailed. A less diligent approach influenced the working of established techniques. Even Louisa Pesel, an important early twentieth century embroiderer, thought creating an effect with design was more important than the quality of the workmanship. For example, the reverse of her apron without strings is surprisingly untidy (No. 87). In contrast, in earlier periods it was acknowledged that an enduring needlework technique developed through trial and error, and the way in which materials were treated contributed to their durability.

Sampler making, too, had lost its impetus. Its nineteenth century use as an educational tool was no longer relevant. In its residual form it became primarily commemorative and celebratory (Nos. 92 and 97) rather than innovative, as in No. 95. Canvaswork remained popular (No. 94), the repertoire of stitches increasing to include those which had originated in other counted work techniques (No. 100).

86. PRINTED SAMPLER. English, 1902.
Stamped plain weave linen; floss and twisted silk. Stitches include long and short, satin and stem. 214 x 650 mm (8.4 x 25.5 in).
Worked in a brilliant silk twist similar to the product manufactured by James Pearsall & Co. Ltd. known as 'Broriche'. Produced to commemorate the coronation of Edward VII, rhyming captions accompany each element, expressing childish sentiments to evoke a bygone era. (Dorset County Museum T1271952-42-2)

87. EMBROIDERED APRON. 'Louisa Pesel'. English, about 1910.
Plain weave linen; linen thread and silk. Stitches include Holbein, stem and cross .
815 x 615 mm (32 x 24.25 in).
Embroidered in the Blackwork technique. A bibbed apron with a large pocket but emblematically lacking apron strings. The principal band pattern is adapted from a mid seventeenth century band sampler (Victoria and Albert Museum No. 829-1902) and an eglantine rose taken from a sampler inscribed 'Isbel Hall, Febrvary 1653' (Mrs Clement Williams Collection, in 1931). The back of the work shows sparse attention to detail. Louisa F. Pesel (*circa* 1870-1947) was President of the Embroiderers' Guild. (Embroiderers' Guild Collection EG2080)

91. EMBROIDERED PICTURE. Constance Ethel Dickinson. English, 1942-45.
Plain weave linen; watercolour paint; twisted cotton. Stitch include cross, satin, chain and French knot. 310 x 245 mm (12.25 x 9.5 in).
An imaginary English cottage embroidered by Constance Dickinson with additional watercolour background details. A nostalgic plume of smoke rises on the air, birds fly over a garden filled with spring flowers. Worked in Changi Prison, Singapore, after Mrs Dickinson and her husband, an Inspector General in the Police, were taken Prisoners of War by the Japanese in 1942. The linen ground was cut from a pair of shorts and the threads carried into prison with commendable *sang froid* by Mrs. Dickinson. After the war the Dickinsons returned to England and bought a cottage remarkably similar to the one she had embroidered. (Mrs Pauline Asbury)

92. *(Opposite page)* CANVASWORK SAMPLER. Mary Fox Pitt. English, 1955.

Canvas weave cotton at 18 threads to the inch; Appleton's crewel wool, stranded cotton and twisted metal purl. Stitches include French knot, tent, reverse tent, Algerian plaited and Algerian eye, straight satin, mosaic. 335 x 205 mm (13.25 x 8.25 in).

Inscribed, 'Sarah Mary Lane Fox Pitt 3rd August 1941'.

Designed and worked in 1955 by Mary Fox Pitt for her daughter Sarah. Each of the motifs has a significance in the life of the dedicatee and was chosen by her; they include family crests, her father and brothers, her ponies and dogs, and a pedigree herd of Guernsey cattle. The corners signify a chess board, tennis racquet, playing cards and her books. (Private Collection)

94. *(Right)* DESIGN FOR A CANVASWORK PANEL. Penny Burns. English, 1959-60.

The panel: canvas weave cotton at 18 threads to the inch; Anchor stranded cotton. Tent stitch. 980 x 323 mm (39 x 12.75 inches).

The illustration shows Penny Burns design for a panel worked by her mother Elizabeth Harter. Influenced by the Berlin wool work panel (No. 82) belonging to her parents, Penny Burns designed the needlepoint panel with an unworked grounding. Victorian panels were available from needlework retailers with the beaded designs worked, leaving the purchaser to fill in the background if required. (Mrs Penny Burns)

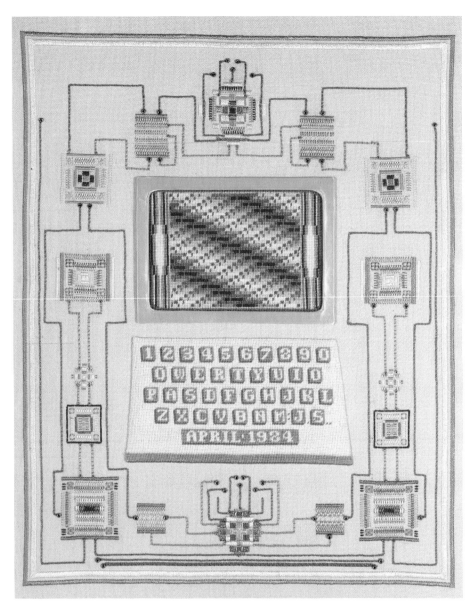

95. SAMPLER. 'Peace'. Joan Syrett. English, 1984.
Canvas weave cotton. Stitches include cross, satin, long and short and straight. 525 x 420 mm (21 x 16.5 in).
A witty and original design, where the format of letters on the keyboard, almost but not quite, repeats that established on typewriters since the mid-nineteenth century, thereby replacing the fixed order of letters of the alphabet normally associated with later samplers. The maker's initials and the date 'J S APRIL 1984' are inscribed following the letter 'M'. Formerly in the possession of Dr Douglas Goodhart, who had a good eye for a sampler. He bequeathed his extensive collection to the National Trust. (Dr. Goodhart Collection, Montacute House, Somerset. The National Trust)

[80]

96. NEEDLEPOINT WAISTCOAT. 'The Dogs'. Sandra Henville. English, 1985.
Canvas weave cotton at 18 threads to the inch; satin weave silk; watercolour paint; glass buttons. Anchor stranded cotton worked in tent stitch. 360 x 475 mm (14.25 x 19 in).

Designed by Paul Sinodhinos, with the canvas painted by Penny Burns. Held on a hand tenter frame, the needlepoint took three months to complete. The same design was repeated and worked for two other waistcoats, one as a companion piece in Appleton's crewel wool, worked in basketweave tent-stitch by Kathleen Dyson for winter wear. (Paul Sinodhinos)

99. RECTANGULAR RAISED WORK BOX. 'Nursery Rhymes'. Beryl Rosemary Lawrence. English, 1993.

Silk weave, calico weave cotton; leather, lurex, wool, cardboard, beads, cording, velvet, wire, pipe cleaners, feathers and sheep's tow. Wood. Stitches include long and short, cross, detached buttonhole, needlelace, French knot, Cretan, turkey work, feather, wheatsheaf, satin and bullion. 180 x 370 x 140 mm (6.5 x 14.5 x 5.25 in).

Designed by Beryl Rosemary Lawrence depicting five nursery rhymes, the children's figures are worked in silk and leather. Inscribed 'Boys and Girls Come Out To Play'. Signed and dated. (Beryl Rosemary Lawrence)

97. *(Opposite page)* SPOT MOTIF MARRIAGE SAMPLER. Julia de Salis. English, 1989.

Plain weave linen; fabric paint, stranded cotton thread. Stitches include satin, stem, slanting gobelin, brick, French knot, lazy daisy, detached floaters and random infillings. 430 x 305 mm (17 x 12 in).

Inscribed 'Maria & Sebastian', the date of the wedding of Maria Scrope and Sebastian Chambers, '8th of July 1989' and 'J de Salis'. Eighteen spot motifs significant to the life of the bride and groom, including a row of young animals in which a baby in a nappy (diaper) comes face to face with a pink pig; enclosed within a border of alternating large and small hearts. (Private Collection)

100. CANVASWORK PICTURE. Merula Salaman. English, 1995.
Canvas weave cotton; Appleton's crewel wool. Stitches include blanket, brick, chain, fly, knitting, loop, with long and short and stem. 298 x 294 mm (11.75 x 11.5 in).
Entitled on the reverse: 'Blackbird swearing at a Cat'.

Adapting a needlepainting technique developed in the 1770s (No. 37), Merula Salaman followed a traditional design format of tree, bird and beast. The format flowered in the early Jacobean period, and may have been developed originally to illustrate Aesop's fables. Merula Salaman was the wife of Sir Alec Guinness. Apart from her needlework pictures, she wrote and illustrated several childrens' books.

Merula is the Latin word for blackbird. We can amuse ourselves by speculating at whom Merula is swearing. (Private Collection)

101. 'MILLENNIUM CASKET'. Barbara and Roy Hirst. English, 1998-2000.
Fibreboard, plywood; calico, bonded silk organza, vilene, wire, mica, brass, leather, feathers, beads, felt, aluminium, silk dyes, paint, stuffing. Stitches include French knot, long stitch floater. Techniques include needlelace, machine embroidery, padded and applied slips and pico edging. 258 x 250 x 194 mm (10 x 9.75 x 7.5 in).
The hipped and raised casket comprises 44 surfaces, each worked from a wide variety of design soruces. The embroidery illustrated was inspired by a medieval manuscript in the British Library of a castle under siege. (Barbara and Roy Hirst)

102. EMBROIDERED BOX. 'The Secret Garden'. Marilyn Wyatt. English, 1999-2000.
Calico, canvas; cardboard, felt, linen, net, nylon, metallic organza, plastic, vanishing fabric, wire; crewel wool, stranded and perle cotton. Stitches include detached buttonhole, chain, bullion and French knot. 25 x 105 x 105 mm (5 x 4.25 x 4.25 in).
Fitted with a lid, the sides drop to reveal a contemporary garden, with a pond, filled with spring and early summer flowers and creatures. (Marilyn Wyatt)

POINTING THE WAY
2001

The organisers of 'The Point of the Needle' Exhibition invited leading British embroiderers to produce original work to be shown in conjunction with the selection of historical embroideries. They were looking for embroidery that would show the vitality of contemporary work and indicate new directions. Participants were encouraged to use any technique and preferably to avoid reproducing a traditional sampler.

The response was vigorous, varied and vital, with entries from men as well as women – a healthy sign in itself. The embroideries are witty and individual, displaying considerable technical expertise. Combined with the work from the closing years of the twentieth century, they leave us assured that the needle is in good hands, and pointing the way forward to whatever unexpected and exciting developments lie ahead.

103. COLLAGE PANEL. 'Morning Glory'. Richard Box, 2001.
Fabric; machine embroidery. 240 x 290 mm (9.5 x 11.5 in).
The painter, embroiderer, and author Richard Box is well-known for his pioneering use of the sewing machine to create colourful and imaginative collages and embroideries. Countless images of his work have been published, and he enthusiastically shares ideas and techniques with fellow embroiderers. (Richard Box)

104. 21ST CENTURY SAMPLER. Created and worked by Rebecca Smith, Rosalinda Bennett, Sarah Prime, Jane Desborough and Sarah Stowger, 2001.

White grounding; polychrome threads and Jap gold. Stitches include back, French knot, satin, stem, raised stem, long and short, split. Techniques include applied work, gold work, hardanger, machine embroidery, needlepoint shading, raised work, and canvaswork. 300 x 275 mm (12 x 11 in).

A group project worked by third year apprentices of the Royal School of Needlework. A 'modern alphabet' with symbols and logos representing each letter, displayed on an image of a computer screen.

A witty and skilfully worked co-operative piece, in which 'a' is the symbol for 'at', 'b' is a barcode, 'c' is the logo of 'Cable & Wireless', 'd' is a dollar sign, 'e' stands for the European Community, 'f' is the symbol for 'female', 'g' stands for 'genetics', 'h' for 'heritage', 'i' for 'Information Centre', 'j' for 'Justice', 'k' for 'Kodak', 'l' for 'Lottery', 'm' for 'Millennium Man', 'n' is the 'Nike' logo, 'o' is the five Olympic rings, 'p' is a Penguin book, 'q' stands for Mary Quant, 'r' is a ribbon, 's' stands for 'Save the Children', 't' is a treble clef, 'u' is the sign for the London Underground, 'v' stands for 'vegetarian', 'w' is the 'Windows' symbol, 'x' stands for 'Exit'. Not showing are the 'y' and 'z'. (Royal School of Needlework)

105. DECORATIVE PANEL. 'The Clothes of the Pearly Princess'. Katriina Hyslop, English, 2001.
Plain weave silk organza. Stitches include back, stem, chain, long and short, Techniques include couching, applied, collage and beadwork. 300 x 320 mm (12 x 12.5 in).
Inspired by the colourful and distinctive outfits worn by the Cockney 'Pearly Kings and Queens'.

Katriina Hyslop was born in 1958, and worked for many years in Edinburgh in the antiquarian book trade, while developing her creative skills making hand-embroidered pictures. She has exhibited frequently in the British Isles and her style is always apposite to her theme, with the result that her work is varied, distinctive and witty. (Katriina Hyslop)

106. *(Opposite page)* FIGURATIVE PANEL. 'Market Day'. Katriina Hyslop, 2001.
Plain weave silk organza. Stitches include long and short, satin. Techniques include couching, applied and raised work. 280 x 180 mm (11 x 7 in).
Contemporary embroiderers like Katriina Hyslop, using the wealth of materials available today, and adapting them to explore raised work, are notable for their use of themes drawn from everyday life. Unlike the young embroiderers of the second half of the seventeenth century who also used raised techniques, the current work is freer and more spontaneous, as embroiderers are no longer dependent on engraved prints for their inspiration. (Katriina Hyslop)

107. SAMPLER. 'Circumnavigator'. Paddy Killer. English, 2001.
Plain weave silk, silk organza; silk and cotton. Techniques include drawing, painting, bonding and machine embroidery. 250 x 100 mm (9.95 x 4 in).
The subject is the yachtsman David Scott Cowper, who is on his fifth solo 'Round the World' voyage, on this occasion circumnavigating the world via the North-east Passage. Of him, Paddy Killer has written: 'I think he must be mad: when I asked him what he wore under his survival gear, he looked at me as if I was mad and said, "Why, a shirt and tie of course", so I had to do a portrait of him.'

Paddy Killer worked in fashion in London and Montreal before embarking on a solo career as a textile artist in 1974. A member of the 62 Group of Textile Artists since 1985, with whom she has exhibited, other major exhibitions in which she has participated include 'Out of the Frame', 'In Arkadia', 'Art Textiles 2' and 'Art of the Stitch'. Paddy Killer is a talented draftswoman with a fine eye. Her style is concise and accurate and her embroideries original and accomplished. (Paddy Killer)

Within image: God is our guide! No swords we draw, / We kindle not war's battle fires, / By reason, union, justice, law, / We claim the birthright of our sires, / We raise the watchword 'Liberty' / We will, we will, we will be free!

Thomas Stan

George Lovel

109. SAMPLER. 'The Tolpuddle Martyrs'. Norman Willis, English, 2001.
Plain weave cotton; D.M.C. stranded cotton. Stitches include straight, long and short, cross. 700 x 400 mm (28 x 16 in).

This detail from the sampler designed by Norman Willis portrays George Loveless, one of the six Dorset labourers from the village of Tolpuddle, who in 1834 were sentenced to transportation for forming the first trades union. Norman Willis writes: 'As the Tolpuddle Martyrs lived near Dorchester, and were tried at Dorchester Court, the idea was a "natural". . . much detailed work (was) carried out by Zoe Halstead, of D.M.C. Some art work by Jack Peppiatt.'

Norman Willis was General Secretary of the Trade Union Council (T.U.C.) 1984-93, and President of the European T.U.C. He is a Trustee and Director of the Royal School of Needlework, and Vice President of the Poetry Society. A writer, broadcaster and lecturer, he is a great enthusiast for stitching. (Norman Willis)

AN ASSORTMENT OF TOOLS.
Including a mid-nineteenth century celluloid pig emery powder holder for cleaning
needles and pins; a Victorian gilded metal etui bird, perched on an egg, containing
six ivory and gilded tools; an ivory, horn and buck pelt scimitar shaped needlecase,
known as the 'Hertfordshire Hind', English, and a Beech needlecase, a hatted
youth, with folded arms standing on a pedestal.

EXHIBITION ENTRIES NOT ILLUSTRATED

1. SAMPLER FRAGMENT. English School, late sixteenth century. *Plain weave linen with polychrome silks. Early unstructured sampler fragment worked with flowers and strawberry spot motifs. 200 x 213 mm (8 x 8.5in).* (Private Collection)

2. WROUGHT SWEET BAG. English School, 1588-1600. *Plain weave linen, polychrome silks and metallic threads. Worked in tent stitch with silver ground. Multi coloured plaited drawstrings. 125 x 125 mm (5 x 5 in).* (Private Collection)

3. PANEL OF SPOT MOTIFS. English School, 1600-1610. *Plain weave linen, polychrome silks, silver and gold metallic threads. Three slips embroidered, with other slips partly worked. 275 x 450 mm (11 x 18 in).* (Private Collection)

13. SATIN PINCUSHION. English School, 1647. *Satin weave silk, floss silk, twisted metal coiled wire wrapped with silk and other metallic thread, with metallic lace edging and spangles. 150 x 100 mm (6 x 4 in).* (Barbara and Roy Hirst)

16. CREWELWORK CURTAIN. English School, 1650-75. *Twill weave linen and cotton; worsted wool. Tampour work. 270 x 1460 mm (10.5 x 58.25 in).* (Private Collection)

17. FLORAL SLIPS. English School, 1650-75. *Canvas-weave linen; silk and silk threads worked in half cross or tent stitch; applied work. 2800 x 1400 mm (112 x 56 in).* (Private Collection)

33. POLE SCREEN FLORAL PANEL. English School, 1750-70. *Plain weave linen with wool in half cross or tent worked horizontally, vertically and diagonally with the dictates of the pattern. 670 x 540 mm (26.25 x 21.25 in).* (Sir Mervyn Medlycott, Bt.)

57. SAMPLER WITH MEANDERING BORDER. 'Mary West'. English School, 1829. *Plain weave tammy with double blue line banded selvedge both left and right edges, polychrome silks. Stitches include buttonhole, chain, cross, long and short, split and stem. 381 x 331 mm (15.25 x 13.25 in).* (Dorset County Museum 1958-7-1)

59. SAMPLER. 'Eliza Wagg'. English School, 1833. *Plain weave linen; silks. Cross and satin stitch. 363 x 362 mm (14.5 x 14.5 in).* (Siva Swaminathan Collection)

60. CHRISTENING CUSHION. 'Phebe Chaddick's work 1835'. English School. *Plain weave tammy; silk covering, silk tassels; polychrome silk thread worked in cross stitch. 175 x 119 mm (7 x 4.5 in).* (Dorset County Museum T75)

70. A PAIR OF BEADED WATCH POCKETS. *Felt, plain-weave silk; silk lining, white and grey glass beads and attached steel hooks. Grisaille pattern of beaded floreate trefoils on scallop shaped pockets. 165 x 165 mm (6.5 x 6.5 in).* (Private Collection).

72-80. PLAIN SEWING ITEMS. Worked, but not all marked by Elizabeth Vickery, 1864-72, both as a pupil at Burlescombe School, Devon, and as a pupil-teacher. They include miniature samplers, spot motifs, specimen patches and a miniature shirt, for which she received a prize. Worked in a wide range of stitch techniques. (Dorset County Museum)

81. A DORCHESTER, WEYMOUTH & CERNE DISTRICT ASSOCIATION CERTIFICATE 1872. Awarded to Elizabeth Vickery. (Dorset County Museum)

82. EMBROIDERED PATCHWORK COVER. Inscripted 'Saml. Green Royal Regiment 1869'. English School. *Plain weave worsted wool; silk. Stitches include chain, long and short and stem. 1690 x 1562 mm (67.5 x 62.5 in).* (Private Collection)

83. BERLIN WOOL WORK BIRD PANEL. English School, about 1870. *Single German plain weave cotton canvas marked in orange every tenth warp thread to assist with counting stitches. Wool with stranded cotton as highlighting. 435 x 435 mm (17.5 x 17.5 in).* (Mrs Penny Burns)

88. PLAIN SEWING SAMPLER. English. Inscribed: 'St. Joseph's School, Taunton' (Somerset) and 'E G 1913'. *Plain weave cotton, silk jersey, plain weave wool; 'nun's cloth', netting; metal hooks and eyelets. A diverse and varied collection of techniques. 1413 x 213 mm (56.5 x 8.25 in).* (Private Collection)

89. EMBROIDERED SILK PANEL. English School, about 1926. *Plain weave silk worked with silk in a variety of embroidered flat stitches. 525 x 550 mm (21 x 22 in).* (Siva Swaminathan Collection)

90. ART DECO POCHETTE. English School, 1930s. Worked by Molly Booker. *Cotton canvas, upholstery fabric lining, polychrome silk. Tent stitch and sloping gobelin. 155 x 262 mm (6 x 10.5 in).* (Embroiderers' Guild Collection EG2661)

93. MONOCHROME SPOT SAMPLER. English School, about 1950. *Plain weave linen, cotton. 355 x 250 mm (14.25 x 10 in).* (Embroiderers' Guild Collection EG924)

98. RAISED WORK BORDER FOR A LOOKING GLASS. Beryl Lawrence. English, 1991. Original design by Barbara Dunhill, taken from Muriel Best *Stumpwork* (Batsford). *Linen/cotton mix, leather, silk weave satin, wool, DMC soft cotton and perlé; lambswool. Oval glass and wooden frame. Techniques: raised and applied canvas work. Stitches include brick, long, satin, lazy daisy, Hungarian, coiled stem and seeding. Frame size: 760 x 660 mm (30.5 x 26.5 in).* (Beryl Lawrence)

108. SAMPLER. 'A Box of Shells'. Belinda Montagu, 2001.
Shells worked in a variety of techniques on a black background. 400 x 300 mm (16 x 12 in). Belinda Montagu is a member of the Mid Wessex Embroiderers' Guild and her commissions include the New Forest Embroidery and Domus Wall Hangings. The shell box is inspired by the collage and paper mosaics of Mrs Delany, an eighteenth century embroiderer and favourite of George III, who favoured black as a background for her botanical designs. (Belinda Montagu)

FURTHER READING

Arnold, Janet, *Queen Elizabeth's Wardrobe Unlock'd* (W.S. Maney), 1988

Best, Muriel, *Stumpwork* (B.T. Batsford), 1987

Clabburn, Pamela, *The Needleworker's Dictionary* (William Morrow & Co), 1976

Colby, Averil, *Samplers* (Batsford), p/b 1987

Davies, Natalie Zemon, *Women on the Margins* (Harvard University Press), 1995

Greer, Germaine, Ed., *Kissing the Rod* (Virago), 1988

Grieve, H.E.P., *Examples of English Handwriting 1150-1750* (Essex Education Committee), 1954

Hackenbroch, Yvonne, *English & other Needlework Tapestries and Textiles* (Irwin Untermyer Collection) (Thames and Hudson, London), 1960

Hughes, Therle, *English Domestic Needlework 1660-1860* (Abbey Fine Arts), n.d.

Huish, Marcus, *Samplers and Tapestry Embroideries* (Dover), Reprint Series

Hutchinson, Lucy, *Memoirs of the Life of Colonel Hutchinson* (Everyman), 1968

Johnson, Eleanor, *Needlework Tools* (Shire Album 38), 1986

Johnstone, Pauline, *Three Hundred Years of Embroidery 1600-1900, Treasures from the Embroiders' Guild Collection* (Wakefield Press), 1986

Laurence, Anne, *Women in England 1500-1760* (Weidenfeld and Nicholson), 1994

Lummis, Trevor & Marsh, Jan, *The Woman's Domain* (Penguin), 1993

Mason, John & Elizabeth, *A Schole-House for the Needle* (reprint of 1632 edition) R.J.L. Smith & Associates, 1998

Parker, Rozsika, *The Subversive Stitch* (Women's Press), 1984

Proctor, Molly G., *Victorian Canvas Work* (Batsford), 1972

Schultz, H.C., *The Teaching of Handwriting in Tudor and Stuart Times* (Huntington Library Quarterly, vi), 1943

Schuette, Marie & Muller, Christensen, Trans. Donald King, *The Art of Embroidery* (Thames & Hudson), 1963

Symonds, Mary & Preece, Louisa, *Needlework through the Ages* (Hodder & Stoughton Ltd), 1928

Synge, Lanto, *Art of Embroidery: History of Style and Technique* (The Royal School of Needlework, Antique Collectors' Club), 2001

Tuer, Andrew W., *The History of the Horn book* (The Leadenhall Press Ltd, London, & EC & Charles Scribner, NY), 2 Vols FSA 1896

Warner, Pamela, *Embroidery, A History* (Batsford), 1991

Wells-Cole, *Art and Decoration in Elizabethan and Jacobean England*, 1997

Wingfield Digby, George, *Elizabethan Embroidery* (Faber & Faber), 1963

CATALOGUES

Arthur, Liz, *Embroidery at the Burrell Collection* (John Murray in Association with Glasgow Museums), 1995

Brooke, Xanthe, *The Lady Lever Art Gallery Catalogue of Embroideries* (Alan Sutton), 1992

Christie's, *An Important Collection of Needlework* (Sir Frederick Richmond Sale), 1987

Coron, Sabine et Lefevre, *Livres de Broderie Reliures francaises du Moyen Age a nos Jours* (B.N. de France Dollfus Mieg et Cie), 1995

Dillmont, Therese de, *Encyclopedia of Needlework*, n.d. 1860-70

Epstein, Kathleen, *British Embroidery: Curious Works from the Seventeenth Century* (The Colonial Williamsburg Foundation, Williamsburg, Virginia, and Curious Works Press, Austin, Texas), 1998

Ewles, Rosemary and Astley-Cooper, Pat, *One Man's Samplers* (The Goodhart Collection), 1983

Ewles, Rosemary and Woolley, Hilary, *The Goodhart Samplers' Exhibition* (Glynn Vivian Art Gallery & Museum), 1985

Jarrett, Joy & Scott, Rebecca Jarrett, *An A-Z of British 18th & 19th Samplers* (Witney Antiques), 1993
    Samplers, All creatures Great and Small (Witney Antiques), 1996
    Samplers, a School-Room Exercise (Witney Antiques), 1994
    Samplers, House and Garden (Witney Antiques), 1995

Jarrett, Joy, Jarrett, Stephen, & Scott, Rebecca, *British Samplers and Historic Embroideries 1590-1880* (Witney Antiques), 1999

Humphrey, Carol, *Samplers* (Fitzwilliam Museum Handbook), 1997

Kendrick A.F., *Catalogue of Samplers* (Victoria and Albert Museum), 3rd ed. 1922

King, Donald, *Samplers* (Victoria and Albert Museum), Crown Copyright 1960

Nevinson, John L., *Catalogue of English Domestic Embroidery of the Sixteenth and Seventeenth Centuries* (HMSO), Reprint 1950
    Some Pictures and Samplers from the Collection of Lady St John Hope (Privately printed at the University Press, Cambridge), 1949

Tarrant, Naomi E.A., *The Royal Scottish Museum Samplers*, 1978

Walton, Karin-M, *Samplers in the City of Bristol Museum and Art Gallery*, 1983

Wardle, Patricia, (with Levey, Santina), *Guide to English Embroidery*, 1970

PHOTOGRAPHIC ACKNOWLEDGEMENTS

I am grateful to the following photographers for the high standard of their work: Paul Lipscombe (Dorset County Museum, some Private Collections), John Baxter (Private Collection), Ian Blantern (National Trust), Dominic Brown (Royal Collection), A.C. Cooper Ltd (Siva Swaminathan Collection), Chris Christodoulou (Royal School of Needlework), Helen Francis (Embroiderers' Guild Collection), Martin Gostelow (Private Collection), Barbara Hirst (Barbara and Roy Hirst), Justin Jarrett (Witney Antiques).